Travellers

We see as we are

A 'Change-ability' title

Steve Unwin

Photon Books
www.photonbooks.com

Published by Photon Books 2008
First published in Great Britain in 2007
www.photonbooks.com

Printed and bound in Great Britain.

ISBN 978-1-906420-01-7

Printed by Biddles, Kings Lynn
www.biddles.co.uk

ATEBIDPC3.0

To Us All

We are not the sum of all that we do,
rather we become the creation of all that we experience.

Other books in the change-ability series

Letting go by Steve Unwin   May 2007.

Other books by Steve Unwin

Essence of Da Vinci

Essence of Change

Prague Inspired

Himalayan Odyssey

Iran Inspired

For more information see page 164.

For news of the latest titles please visit,

www.photonbooks.com

Contents

Acknowledgements

Writing appears to be both a solitary and a slow process. Whilst solitude is required, it is perhaps its slowness that holds its secret. The pace of writing forces the writer to step outside the daily routine, focus and slow down the processes of thought. When we do, we quieten the ongoing drumbeat of our lives, and allow space for reflection and thinking.

We may believe that this enables our innate ability to surface, and in part it must, but there is a paradox in the isolation of the writer. When we sit alone, we allow the infinite connections we have with others to come into focus. The world the writer is drawn into in creating their work, may sit entirely within their head, but it is not a solitary place. It is a world richly populated with experience, chance encounters, conversations, shared phrases, thoughts and ideas. To write is

'There is not any present moment that is unconnected with some future one. The life of every man is a continued chain of incidents, each link of which hangs upon the former. The transition from cause to effect, from event to event, is often carried on by secret steps, which our foresight cannot divine, and our sagacity is unable to trace. Evil may at some future period bring forth good; and good may bring forth evil, both equally unexpected.'
Joseph Addison

to draw upon all of these connections, and all of the interactions with the people and events around us, and in our pasts and our futures.

These contacts are sometimes formal or prolonged, but often may be brief and barely noticed. Their value may have been glimpsed at the time, or may only be visible months or years later.

To write is thus to describe not one's own understanding or discoveries, but to serve as a channel through which to reveal our collective understanding. Though in a real sense this understanding is what we all already know, this knowledge is often so deeply buried that we might live a lifetime without acknowledging its presence. However, it sits within all of us.

I would like to thank everyone who has contributed, often unknowingly to the writing process. I hope that the resulting book will serve to stimulate many new connections, which you will value and enjoy.

Extra special thanks to my family for their support, love and understanding, without which nothing is possible, and to Mary T Tierney for her inspiration.

Steve Unwin
July 2008.

Change-ability

Change is a feature of all of our lives. Indeed we might reasonably say that it is change that defines the presence of life, from the beat of our heart to the gradual ageing in our body. These changes, whether welcome or not, happen at a level below our consciousness. However when the need for change becomes a conscious one, we may find that we fear its effects, and seek the means to avoid or simply ignore it.

We find ourselves a decade later, still in the temporary job we took, or with DIY tasks left undone for months or even years.

'Too often we...
enjoy the comfort of
opinion without the
discomfort of
thought.'
John F. Kennedy

We look for comfort in standing still, but our world continues to move. And when change can no longer be avoided, we accept the need, often with ill grace, and may feel we are coping with what life throws at us. We deny change's

'You have to leave the city of your comfort and go into the wilderness of your intuition. What you'll discover will be wonderful. What you will discover is yourself.'
Alan Alda.

inevitability, and instead see an unwanted intrusion to our otherwise stable lives. With little thought, other than to re-create this false sense of stability, we deal with change using ready made solutions. Yet however good they are, these are solutions that worked in a world that no longer exists, a world swept aside by change's relentless march.

When we think in this way of change destroying the past, we naturally feel like victims of its actions. If instead we can see it as creating the space for tomorrow, then we begin to embrace its energy and potential.

Whilst the past is a place of answers and the false comfort of certainty, the future is explored with questions. It's a place where nothing is certain, and thus everything possible.

Change-ability Series

Each book in the change-ability series, rather than providing a jig-saw puzzle piece of prescribed knowledge, instead offers to stimulate ideas that may form part of the mosaic of your own understanding. I hope you enjoy your journey through the book.

If you would like to share your comments and thoughts I would love to hear from you. Please email travellers@photonbooks.com.

Introduction

'No amount of measurement of the acorn will reveal anything about the oak tree within it.'
Steve Unwin

I hope you will enjoy and value this book, but to do this I invite you to make the book your own. I'd like you to annotate the text, add your comments and thoughts, delete and underline, whatever is required to turn this from my book into yours.

Let me explain why.

At the heart of change-ability is the idea that change isn't something that we do, but is instead something we are being.

I admit that to many this might appear a rather subtle or obtuse distinction; aren't we what we do?

More than this, changing what we are, seems a rather intangible and nebulous goal. It has none of the immediacy, clarity and focus that lends itself to changing something we do.

A decision to do something, to quit smoking, begin exercising, enrol for a class, the list goes on but they all have the comforting feel of being something you can write on a calendar and circle. Next Wednesday I begin at the gym. I'll have started writing my memoirs by this time next week. I'll pick up the children at four o'clock. They all have a neat point in time when they'll be undertaken or completed.

Now clearly there's a place for these things. We need to pick up the children by four, or they'll be left at school. If we're ever going to write that book, then we need to sit down and type the first word. Even if we hurriedly erase it, retype and erase again, we've made a start. There is no problem with these things per se, but this is a book about change.

Now you may well argue that each of these actions is precisely about change. The blank piece of paper, or empty computer screen, is changed by that first word. .

I confess that I can't argue against this; however what we want to think about is a little different.

When we do each of these things, what we are actually trying to achieve is something rather bigger. When we go to the gym, its part of getting ourselves fit. When we pick up the children from school, we are loving them, caring for them, nurturing them, helping them develop and grow.

Of course, you can quite rightly say that everything is part of something else, and that the distinction I'm drawing is again an imagined one. But I'd like to suggest that there is an important difference, important if we are going to think about change.

The comfort we get from doing things isn't just the circled date in the calendar, or time slot in our schedule. When we do things, they get done. There is nothing vague. The children were either picked up or not, and there's a wonderful permanence to it. If you picked them up, then they stay picked up, even if you have to repeat the task the next day. Each instance, if done, stays done. Time doesn't pick at your accomplishment, seeking to undo it.

When we deal with doing things, we live in this wonderful world of certainty. We either succeeded or we didn't. And our success or failure is then permanently framed in the past.

We love this certainty, indeed we crave it so much so that colours the way we see the world. Instead of a dynamic swirling whirlpool of change, opportunity and happenings now, we see the world through static slices of the past. The individual frames of a movie film.

'Madame, there are always two paths to take; one back towards the comforts and security of death, the other forward to nowhere.'
Henry Miller

Often, just as in the movie film, these individual frames are barely distinguishable from one another. Each day bares the imprint of the previous one. Today rather than being new, becomes an extension of yesterday.

Think for a moment of how different, or not, your day at work was today, compared with a day a year ago. When did you last eat at a new restaurant, or chose something unknown from the menu? When did you read a book you didn't think you'd like, talk with people you would normally avoid, or listen to a new type of music for the first time.

These feel like things to do, but we're looking for something different. Rather than a list of steps to take, we want to think about the nature of walking to get at the essence of real change.

To do so we have to step away from this sense of certainty. We can know with certainty that we picked up the children, but if instead we take the dynamic perspective and consider the degree to which we are nurturing them, then we move into areas that are much more difficult to measure, and which lack that comforting certainty of being discrete past events.

Every moment of one's existence one is growing into more or retreating into less.
Norman Mailer

When we consider nurturing we are inevitably drawn into considering a continuous process. There is no end point. Whilst we could describe discrete nurturing events, we are invited to move beyond this into the dynamic world of real change. A world in which we become a nurturer, we love, we are.

Now we glimpse the reality of what I believe to be real change. Change is continuous. The terms continuous improvement or continuous change are tautologies. Real change has a characteristic that transcends events, transcends things that are done. We may go to the gym, but we become fit when a real change takes place within us, in the way we are.

Of course it's much easier to agree to visit the gym, circle the diary date, and turn up on time. But to change what we are, is the real benefit, the objective and the real evidence of change.

We face a challenge. This fondness for the simplicity of 'things to do' is not confined to our home lives. At work we see the world through this same mindset. We seek to do things, launch campaigns, introduce initiatives or begin projects in order to deliver improvement. Often these create the comforting noise of something being done, and give the feeling that change is taking place, but all too often their impact is temporary. For a while they change the coat being worn, but do nothing to change the wearer.

This difference between doing and being is a critically important one and sits at the heart of change-ability, but can often appear indistinct.

The reason it is so difficult to see is that it is rather more the product of 'how we see', than of 'what we see'. Doing and being are entwined by the way we see them, but they are different and their difference is important to our understanding of change.

Imagine the painter who focuses on the brush. Of course the brush is key to creating the painting, and until the painter does something with the brush the canvas remains bare, but the magic is not in the paintbrush. If we watch all we will see are paint strokes being applied to the canvas.

In the painters hands the paintbrush disappears and simply becomes the connection between the painter and the painting. The painter is being an artist, not copying or mimicking the actions of one. And for the artist, the paintbrush becomes the means to connect to

'Clay is moulded to make a vessel, but the utility of the vessel lies in the space where there is nothing. ... Thus, taking advantage of what is, we recognize the utility of what is not.'
Lao Tze

'If you don't live it, it won't come out your horn.'
Charlie Parker

'Everything, men, animals, trees, stars, we are all one substance involved in the same terrible struggle. What struggle? ....
Turning matter into spirit.' Zorba scratched his head (and said) 'I've got a thick skull boss, I don't grasp these things easily. Ah if only you could dance all that you've just said, then I'd understand... Or if you could tell me all that in a story boss.'
Nikos Kazantzakis, Zorba the Greek

the painting. For the artist the paint strokes are a side effect of being, not the focus of doing.

But this is not a question of art. Consider a marathon runner, a world champion athlete.

Marathon runners travel 26 miles in less than three hours. They run, and keep running, placing one foot in front of the other, time and again, perhaps forty or fifty thousand times in the race. Watch a video of them in action and you'll see that's what they do. But whilst no doubt there are good and bad ways of putting a foot in front of the other, that's not where the magic of being a great marathon runner lies.

We may slow the video of them running as much as we choose, freeze the frame, zoom in and out and it's all to no avail. The video won't reveal the magic, frozen or slowed down. The magic is somewhere else. We're looking at what the runner does, but to see the magic we need to see in new ways.

Of course we might look for their secret in the training regime, or the diet they follow, but again our focus is on what they do, and again I suggest we will fail to see the magic. It's not that you are looking in the wrong place, but looking in the wrong way.

Their focus is not on taking each of those 50,000 steps. (Just try thinking deeply about how to take a single step and what was once a natural action soon becomes stilted and robotic.) They are being a marathon runner. What they do becomes a side effect of being, not their focus.

The challenge we spoke of earlier is not to visit a new restaurant, read a new book or listen to unfamiliar music. Not to-do a list of tasks, rather it is to become the sort of person who does these things and a thousand others so naturally that it goes unnoticed.

The paradox is that when you have this change-ability, you may or not read new books and listen to new music, and whether you do or not will be of little significance. When you are being, what you do isn't the focus.

When we look to learn from what the successful have done, we are looking in the wrong way. There should be little surprise that so often our efforts achieve so little.

Perhaps now you sense the division between doing and being. At one and the same time it may appear the merest of hairline cracks, glimpsed only when we give it great focus of attention. Yet at any moment it may open as a chasm separating two wildly different ways of seeing and understanding our world.

The aim of this book is that we jointly explore this difference, yet even as we begin, this division is part of our world and will govern how we begin.

As you hold this book you may feel you have something to do; the task of reading. Of course you have, but in a sense not. I would like you to go beyond reading, to being changed by having read. As the author, this takes me from the certain and comfortable ground of counting numbers of books read, and into the continuous process of change of the reader.

As the reader, you are also invited to step from the comforting ground of something to do, towards the continuous process of being. There is an undoubted attraction of seeing this book with a neat ordered start point, and equally neat conclusion. A task that can be completed and then consigned into the certainty of the past.

If it is to become more than a description of ideas about change, and instead become part of the living process of change, then I invite you to bring the book to life by transforming it from my book, into your book. A book that carries your living, developing, changing understanding.

I am of course acutely aware that in making this transformation, it might seem that I'm simply suggesting something to do. But I ask

'We all write
poems; it is simply
that the poets are
the ones who write
in words.'
John Fowles

you, rather than a task to complete, think of this as an invitation to explore, an offer of the freedom to let your mind wander where it chooses.

I hope the book might prompt this exploration. I've chosen quotations for their resonance and you will find that the sources are varied, illuminating connections to the arts, the sciences, humanities, politics and elsewhere.

The margins are wide where you can capture your thoughts in scribbles or sketches so that the book becomes the stimulus for your unique journey.

Travellers

Travelling

The train was late, stopped again, another problem. Jim scanned out of the carriage window, up towards the engine, then back towards the rear. No sign of anything happening. 'Typical' he thought to himself, 'a long journey after a long day in a long week. Why today? Why Friday?'

He didn't need this. He just wanted to be home so he could relax. He had a briefcase full of papers by his feet. He couldn't face them at the moment, and knew they'd occupy Saturday morning, but after that, the chance to take it easy. More pressingly, before that the chance for a drink and some time with his wife. He'd eaten on the train, and his two children would be asleep, but at least the chance of a drink before

'Disconnecting from change does not recapture the past. It loses the future'.
Kathleen Norris

11

bed. The chance to be home. The chance to relax and rest.

Business was busy, no frantic. Things were going well; there were plenty of orders, and lots of work, perhaps too much. Certainly his wife thought so. But more orders meant more work so this must be good. The industry had seen difficult times. The fate of closure had befallen some of the competition, and always seemed to be lurking menacingly not far in the background.

'In all affairs it's a healthy thing now and then to hang a question mark on the things you have long taken for granted.'
Bertrand Russell

Sometimes he felt as if great invisible dice were being rolled, with their result arbitrarily condemning a business to extinction, or signalling survival or success.

Clearly more work was good, but why does business being good often feel so bad? A paradox that crossed Jim's mind from time to time, but usually only briefly as it was soon overtaken by the need to address the work, rather than the apparent extravagance of wondering about its nature.

'Our lives improve only when we take chances - and the first and most difficult risk we can take is to be honest with ourselves.'
Walter Anderson

Glancing at his watch he realised that he'd been on the train for nearly three hours. For a while he'd worked through the papers, tried to, reading, scratching out his thoughts and comments. Meetings to come and meetings past. They'd eventually blurred into one, and he'd reached the point where he recognised words, but couldn't string them together to create any meaning. Had he dozed off? He wasn't sure. Perhaps so, as he didn't recognise the man sitting opposite him across the small Formica covered table that separated them, a table littered with the packaging for food, much of which he equally didn't recognise.

A little younger than Jim, maybe ten years younger and listening to music, an iPod it looked like. He caught Jim's eye and spoke as he removed the earphones.

"Not a good night."

"No." Jim replied. Cupping his hand against the window he strained to look out towards the front of the train.

"Can't see any problem. Can't see much of anything at all really."

Though this was a long summer's day, dusk had now begun to settle. Jim peered into the murky twilight, and thought to himself, 'another week chalked up'.

"You make this journey often?" asked the stranger.

"Every Friday, well most Fridays, unless I'm away. Down on Monday and back on Friday."

After a brief pause during which his new acquaintance remained silent, Jim glanced at his watch before adding, "Looks like it will be well after 11 tonight."

"Before you get home?"

"Yes. Hopefully my wife will be waiting up for me."

"Not so bad for me. I get off at the next stop... though that could be after 11 at this rate! Seems to happen quite a lot; breakdowns, problems and the like. Always seems worse on Fridays"

"Yes you're right."

They shared a smile as the exchange seemed to decide whether to end at a brief shared comment, or to develop further.

The stranger took the initiative.

"You travel for business?"

Business   This was a question that hardly needed asking. Even ignoring the pattern of travel, Jim wore his business life like a badge of office, from his neatly set tie, to his polished shoes, via his reasonably smart grey business suit.

"Yes." Jim's brief reply was not an intentional sign of terseness. He was thinking.

For Jim the task of identification wasn't so easy. He tried to piece together the snippets of accent, the manners and mannerisms and the style of dress. Visible was a smart but casual shirt and a loosely fitting jumper, a round clean shaven face with longish hair, perhaps a little too long by Jim's close cropped standards. For a moment he ran suggestions through his mind as a puzzle. There was little to go on, perhaps he saw something in the face, and maybe the hands. He looked for an answer.

Jim had always admired people who could pinpoint accents and locate someone's place of birth, with what to him appeared an uncanny accuracy. This was a skill with which he was not endowed, but as an alternative he found himself drawn to diagnosing people and situations. If nothing else it helped to while away long journeys. If he cared to admit it, it was a habit that had begun to extend well beyond journeys, and into other parts of his day-to-day routine.

He scanned around the carriage as he thought to himself. 'The lady with the red hat, she's been to a show, and in the bag she's carrying…?'

He thought for a moment. 'Well of course there's the programme from the show, and a gift for her husband. He didn't accompany her, not his sort of show, the ballet perhaps, but he didn't want her to miss it. The man wearing the rugby shirt, he picked that up at the World Cup. Travelled with a party of friends, rowdy friends, wealthy but rowdy. Played rugby at school; went to a top university, Cambridge perhaps. Now starting his career as...' He considered the options and then, pleased with the product of his ruminations, concludes; 'looks like something to do with the legal profession, that's it, destined for politics eventually.'

Of course the reality of these imagined histories was seldom tested, so Jim built a blossoming picture of absolute competence in his diagnostic powers.

He turned over the snippets of evidence surrounding his new acquaintance and the resulting options, and after some seconds of deliberation he announced his verdict.

"And you," he paused, perhaps for effect, or maybe to seek some last minute confirmation.

"I'd think... some kind of an artist," another pause as he draws together the last threads of evidence to determine the fine detail, "maybe a painter, a visual artist anyway."

The stranger gave the slightest of chuckles. Raised eyebrows gave just a hint of surprise, and after a moment of reflection he replied,

"I guess you're right."

The Artist

Jim was not prone to see, far less explore any caveat in the answer or its delivery. His diagnostic prowess had simply been confirmed, with much less need for comment than that the sun's rising confirms another new day.

With the confirmation, Jim now saw the stranger's jumper was a little baggier, and his hair a little more tousled and unkempt, and those hands, yes they were an artist's hands, soft with long slender fingers. They held paintbrushes not spanners and wrenches, not even the pens and pencils that for a long time had served as the tools for Jim's work. A painter's hands.

Jim warmed to the welcome chance to chat, and to someone he had already begun to know, an artist, yes a painter.

'Clever people seem not to feel the natural pleasure of bewilderments, and are always answering questions when the chief relish of life is to go on asking them.'
Frank Moore Colby

"What sort of pictures do you paint?"

Before allowing the time for an answer, he continued with his own.

"I hope it's not this modern stuff," and added as if to answer an unasked question, "I can't understand it."

His involuntary facial contortions underlined his feeling of distaste.

"Oh I can see that", responded the artist. "Why's that?"

Jim leafed through the portion of the discarded food packaging that he did recognise, whilst he answered.

"Well most of it doesn't look like anything. I mean you just can't recognise what it's meant to be a picture of, most of the time."

He spoke as if confident that any sane man could only agree with this view, and had already judged that his new acquaintance fell into the category of the sane.

Portrait   "Now a portrait. I can understand a portrait… or a landscape," Jim continued. "There you can see what's being done. I mean you can tell whether it's been done well or not."

Jim found nothing the least bit tempting amongst the plastic detritus of the table top, and set about crumpling it into a ball in his cupped hands. As he did so he became aware of the contrast between the hands of the artist and the rugged shape of his own.

He scanned around looking for a waste bin, and failing to see one set the ball of packaging on the table. The tightly bound bundle began slowly to extend itself, seeking to take up its designed shape, like the wings of a butterfly freshly released from the confines of the chrysalis. For a moment they were both drawn into watching its slow creaking progress.

"Done well? In what way?" asked the artist eventually inviting Jim to continue.

The answer seemed self evident to Jim, but he accepted the prompt as a courtesy, serving simply to keep the conversation going.

"Well obviously, if you recognise the person who's been painted, without being told, then it's a pretty good test. I mean it must be a pretty good picture."

"Well perhaps a good representation of what they look like?"

The underlying question in the tone of the artist's response was missed, and Jim merely heard confirmation.

"Yes, that's it exactly; if the portrait looks like the person," he nodded to himself as he added "and recognising them is a good clear test."

Jim thought for a moment whilst he stared out of the window, before continuing to elaborate his views. Pointing into the darkening distance, lit by the reflected reddening rays of the departing sun, and already dotted with clusters of man-made light, he added,

'A lady visited Matisse in his studio. Inspecting one of his latest works she unwisely said: 'But surely the arm of this woman is much too long.' 'Madame,' the artist politely replied, 'you are mistaken. This is not a woman, this is a picture.'

"It's the same with a landscape. You don't have to recognise the exact place of course, but if it looks realistic, like the sort of place that could exist, that you could have seen, then it's good."

The artist nodded gently to indicate understanding, and Jim once more saw agreement as he swept his hand across the table top to remove an assortment of crumbs. His cleaning task was now completed, save for the unfurled packaging, which had adopted the role of impromptu decorative tabletop centrepiece, and two long neglected cups of coffee.

There was a brief pause before the artist responded,

"And you?"

Jim's puzzled look prompted the addition of, "Your business?"

Century

"Oh yes. It's not *my* business. My great grandfather started it… well nearly a hundred years ago."

Though established by his great grandfather and still bearing the family name, the company has changed hands since. No longer truly a family firm, Jim has had to work hard to move up through the ranks. He'd begun on the shop floor and progressed on merit, if not to a position at the very top, to a position near enough to reflect a real sense of achievement. He felt aggrieved when people assumed otherwise.

"A hundred years. That's a long time to be in business. There aren't so many companies that last as long as that. What's the secret?"

Though many would have heard the sense of genuine admiration in the artist's words, Jim had perhaps already discounted their value. He'd already judged that the artist would know little of business. He consequently gave little real thought to his reply, other than to maintain the amiable discussion.

"Oh I don't know really. We make good products and our prices are competitive. Just the standard kind of stuff that makes any business successful."

The artist sensed that Jim was less interested in sharing his knowledge of business than in sharing his views on art, but gently pressed to find out more.

"The company must have seen some big changes during that time."

"Oh yes, plenty. I don't know if my great grandfather would recognise the place if he saw it now."

"Big changes?"

"For sure. We've got some pictures taken in the twenties and it's like peering into another world. We've grown over the years, but I like to think that we've not lost the original feeling of being a family firm."

"So you don't have some special ingredient, a secret recipe or some high tech equipment that makes you successful?"

"You mean like Coca Cola, or that fried chicken recipe?" replied Jim.

"That's it, where you each know only part of the ingredients."

"And you're not allowed to all travel on the same aircraft, for fear the secret will be lost forever if it crashes."

"That's the sort of thing."

The artist added playfully, "I think you're safe travelling on the same train, especially slow ones!"

"Stationary ones!" added Jim.

As if provoked by the comment, there was a loud clanking noise and the carriage lurched backwards a little before settling back to rest.

"Careful, it heard you," the artist joked.

Jim peered into the blackness and could see nothing to account for the lurch.

"Perhaps they're coupling up a new engine," he offered as his diagnosis of the noise and bump.

The artist nodded and this prompted Jim to resume his description.

"No business isn't really like that."

Understanding It was clear to Jim that his acquaintance had little understanding of the realities of business, and why should he? He found this lack of understanding tiresome when he was forced to deal with people who he felt ought to know better. Occasionally he'd had to talk to the local press looking for news stories, in search of a headline. He'd sometimes tried to promote good news, a new product launch or the like, but they always seemed more interested in bad news. A minor oil leak that seeped into a local stream, had received more column inches than three year's product launches added together. That, and any hint of job losses seemed to be what sold their papers.

Then there were the local politicians, the M.P. and local councillors who seemed no less fickle than the press, only these were in search of good news. Appearing as uninvited guests when there might be credit to be gained from doing so, and just like the press, always leaving before really understanding anything of the business. But the artist was excused. He had no reason to know.

As he consciously acknowledged this, Jim found himself embellishing his answer.

"No, all the companies, the competition, have pretty much the same equipment. Of course new things do come along, but even if you get in first, within six months everyone is using the same. Word soon gets around."

After a sip from a now bleakly cold cup of coffee, which managed to taste even worse than it had when hot, Jim added in summary.

'At Sony, we assume all products of our competitors will have basically the same technology, price, performance and features.
Design is the only thing that differentiates our product from another in the marketplace.'
Norio Ohga

"No, you can't afford to be left behind, you have to keep up with equipment, new materials, that sort of thing, but it doesn't really give you an advantage."

The artist picked up and peered into his own coffee cup. The far from appetising view meant he risked not even a sip.

"But you must have something, some reason why you've been successful for a hundred years." prodded the artist.

"Ninety-eight."

"Nearly a hundred years."

Jim had been set thinking, but not about the question, rather about the reasons for the artist's apparent interest in the business. He met many people, including the politicians and press, who seemed to him to be happy in their ignorance. When they asked questions they seemed a form of polite entertainment. They passed the time, but for Jim the very fact that they were asked, was evidence that they would not learn from being told. He'd reasoned that they would have had many opportunities to learn, and if they didn't know the answer already, then they wouldn't gain it simply by being told it.

'If you're trying to find something, it means you haven't got it. And if you find it simply by looking for it, that means it's false.'
Pablo Picasso

Relevance

He'd concluded, without really understanding why, that for most people business was something that simply didn't really interest them, or they didn't see as relevant. It was something that was distant from their day to day world. Perhaps this was the case with the artist. His interest was simply idle curiosity.

As he looked across and saw the artist peering into the darkness, nose to nose with his reflection, he allowed his mind to wander a little and place himself in the artist's shoes. Maybe he was truly interested, even intrigued to get a glimpse into a world of not just painting what you see, pictures of what others had created, recording what others have achieved, but instead

'Choose a job you love, and you will never have to work a day in your life.'
Confucius

a world of really doing, of making something. Perhaps this was the attraction.

Jim's thought was interrupted as the artist turned to ask,

"So if I was to paint a picture of your business what would I paint?"

Jim assumed the question was prompted by the artist's examination of the distant silhouetted landscape. As such, it served simply as confirmation of what he saw as the void between the artist's world of disconnected and distant observation, and his real world of the hard nosed reality of doing. Theirs was a world, he reasoned, where you sat outside business, indeed outside any real work, with no need to get involved in understanding, far less actually having to get things done. You had to deal only with the superficial level of how things appeared.

At one and the same time Jim was proud to be distant from that world, and also envious of it. His thoughts spanned the sense of achievement he felt at what he'd done, the progress he'd made, but also what he saw as the cost.

'I wouldn't be working through papers on Saturday morning if I were a painter, that's for sure', he thought to himself.

Idea

Jim's momentary distraction prompted the question to be repeated, "What would a picture of your business look like?"

The question provided Jim with little reason for enthusiasm. He saw no attraction in being drawn into the artist's world. The attraction if any was simply the promise of respite from the pressures of his own; what he new to be the real world. As he saw it, the artist's world was altogether softer and easier, a world of doing as you please, free of deadlines and demands, but with little connection to reality. However he recognised that his real world would have to wait, suspended for the moment as he sat trapped in the train carriage. Despite its recent lurch it remained stubbornly stationary and the conversation would help the time pass. Who knows, he could steer it around to something interesting soon enough, without appearing impolite. He chipped in a response.

'The wise man doesn't give the right answers, he poses the right questions.'
Claude Lévi-Strauss

"Well it could be a picture of our office block."

The artist was quick to respond. "Isn't that just a picture of where you work?"

"Well it's the most picturesque part of the business. The factory is out the back, but it just looks like a huge oversize shed, red brick with a corrugated roof. Not pretty at all. The office block sits at the front of the site."

"But?"

"It's quite an old building, small but at least with a little character. Small leaded windows and even has some ornate columns on a kind of porch at the front."

Sensing from the artist's puzzled expression that his description was not being met with total approval, Jim was driven to embellish his description as best he could.

"In Autumn it actually looks very pretty. There are several large oak and maple trees nearby, and with golden leaves on the ground it makes it look like some grand spot in the country, instead of the cul-de-sac it is, sat in the middle of town."

From the artists puzzled expression it was clear to Jim that he'd still failed to hit the mark, and he continued to delve for an answer that would solicit the artist's approval.

"It's really not much more than an old house attached to the front of the factory, but maybe you could include the trees, move them a little to frame the building. That would make the place look a lot more grand, and still be recognisable."

Workplace

"It sounds nice, but whatever building I paint, it's still just a picture of where you work?" responded the artist, for the first time outlining the cause of his unease.

After a moments thought and analysis, Jim responded.

"Oh I see, yes, well you mean a picture of some of the people."

Jim had quickly diagnosed what he saw as the artist's concern. Yes the thought of adding people felt like a good one. It wouldn't do to have a picture of the business that excluded the people. It wasn't that he'd thought they should be excluded, he just hadn't really felt the need to think too deeply about the question. His mind wandered for a moment as he imagined the employees lined up outside the building, in dappled sunlight framed by the golden sheathed boughs of the trees. The idealised image that came to mind seemed surprisingly pleasing. It wasn't the reality, nor exactly deceitful, just not quite the reality. But it captured something attractive about the business.

Perhaps it was a memory from something in the papers he'd been reading earlier, but the seeds of an idea had suddenly begun to germinate.

"Yes, you could include them in the painting. In fact a picture of people lined up outside the building, a kind of team picture. That would look good." Jim nodded to himself as he spoke, "It would show the personal side of the business, and our people would like to feel involved."

The artist remained silent as the idea grew within Jim and began to envelop him like a warm glow.

"Yes that's a better idea when I come to think of it." Jim pieced together his thoughts as they connected and the idea began to take shape. The artist's question of what a painting may look like had now been reshaped and took the form of an invitation for action.

'Freedom from the desire for an answer is essential to the understanding of a problem.'
J. Krishnamurti

The papers he'd been reading earlier; the forthcoming centenary; a picture of the business. His mind ran on for a few seconds as he thought through an idea, a solution. A picture of the business could be just what he needed. Suddenly this detached discussion of a picture, had snapped into place in his real world. In an instant it had become part of his reality. A reality he now began to share with the artist.

"In eighteen months time it will be our centenary. We could give everyone a print of the painting with themselves in the picture."

He continued to build the idea as he spoke.

"And we could have it turned into Christmas cards as well. Yes that would be a good way to celebrate and save the problem of choosing a card."

Jim added, as if sharing a dark secret, "You wouldn't believe the debates we have" he quickly corrects himself, "arguments we have, about choosing the company Christmas Card!"

In his mind's eye the painting brought a touch of class to the special centenary Christmas Card, class that he felt had been sorely absent from some of the recent year's selections.

Jim pursued his line of thinking, mulling over the thought of how this idea would be greeted back at work, oblivious to the somewhat perplexed expression of the artist.

His colleagues had talked several times about the upcoming centenary. Everyone was keen that something was done, but no one had found the time to sit and think of anything specific. As a result they kept putting off discussion for another day. In the minutes of the latest management meeting this had been succinctly captured, in the mischievous renaming of the celebration as the Centenary Procrastination.

Now his mind raced with other spin off ideas. Perhaps the annual calendar issued to customers could feature the painting. He imagined the calendar in his mind's eye and saw close-ups of individuals for each month, or perhaps pictures of teams and departments. No, he wasn't sure that would work. Whatever, a painting seemed like the answer. He felt a glow of satisfaction when he imagined presenting the idea to his colleagues on Monday. They'd have questions of course. He'd have to think of any potential problems and costs, yes of course he'd have to consider costs, but he felt happy that the hard part of working out what to do was now done.

Jim emerged from his thoughts, still blind to the reaction of the artist.

'If they can get you asking the wrong questions, they don't have to worry about the answers.'

Thomas Pynchon

"They wouldn't have to actually stand there would they?" he asked tentatively in a move to resolve a potential flaw, as he ran through the steps of the plan he had in mind.

"Sorry?" The artist again gently signalled his confusion, but again to no effect.

"I mean they wouldn't have to actually stand in front of the building to be painted? The people? It's not really practical. It's a road, well a turning loop really, but cars and deliveries are coming and going, post, that sort of thing."

"I imagine that it would be done from photographs", the artist replied, beginning to understand now the scope of what he didn't understand.

"Yes of course, photographs."

Photograph The artist would paint the picture from photographs, of course. Jim felt a momentary tinge of embarrassment. Had he really been thinking that the artist would set up his easel outside the factory? Anyway, no matter; he'd assumed no knowledge of business by the artist, so he could readily excuse his lack of knowledge of the artist's trade. He fleshed out his conclusion.

"We could do that early one morning maybe, perhaps in two sessions," he said as he thought through the emerging proposal. If it were two sessions, could the people be painted as one group, kind of mixed together?"

Piece by piece, the challenges of logistics were falling into place for Jim. They'd have to make sure someone manned the phones whilst each photo was taken, and... no, he had it; brilliant; they'd do it as a fire drill. Everyone has to congregate at the front of the building anyway, 'take the picture and capture two birds with one stone' he thought, and smiled to himself at how sweetly his plan was coming together. That was, until the artist interrupted his reverie adding definition to the reasons for his discomfort.

"I think you miss my point. The painting would still just be the place of work and the people who work there."

For Jim the conversation had moved from the idle chatter of discussion, to a piece of work with plans, objectives and an approach. It had now taken the form of a project, his project. He could see how his plan would work, and work well, but the artist still seemed only to be playing with the idea.

Jim heard the artist's comment as a statement of the obvious. It felt less an invitation to continue the discussion, than a potential challenge to his plan, and this perhaps explained the hint of frustration in his response.

"Yes the people and place of work," he confirmed, though the artist's question nagged away at him. Concluding that the artist was simply looking for some sort of elaboration Jim set to thinking what this might mean, and again found himself toying with a stray fragment of the packaging waste as he did so, stretching a piece of plastic film, and watching it curl up when released.

Maybe it was the alliteration in the question that prompted it, but he soon had the answer.

P.P.P.   "Place of work, People... and Products! That was what was missing; of course the products." He instantly built on the new idea by adding to his description.

"Around the side of the painting could be the key products."

He drew circles in the air as he imagined a series of small inset pictures, each one framing a small painting of a product. His thinking ran on for a moment. Perhaps a picture of the services they provided as well. That was it! Products alone wouldn't do it, there weren't enough, but if they included the main services they could have twelve small inset pictures, one for each month. That way it could be used for the company calendar as well. 'Yes, that was a much better idea' he thought.

"Each month of the calendar would feature a product or service," he explained as he began to share his new conclusion with the artist.

His idea now began to feel whole and fully formed. As he savoured the thought, a smile spread across his lips. He could hear the praise already. In one fell swoop he'd addressed the centenary celebration, the Christmas cards and calendar. Perfection!

Jim could see the refreshment trolley being pushed towards him down the carriage. In celebratory mood he announced,

"Let's have a drink, what's your choice; whisky, wine?"

"You don't have to."

"Aw, come on."

"Well, coffee will be just fine thanks," replied the artist.

"Sure?"

"Yes, sure."

"Two coffees." Jim ordered the drinks as he imagines them being delivered in centenary coffee cups, emblazoned with small copies of the company painting.

As he takes the cup he visualises the complete suite of centenary items; employees, customers, suppliers, all their needs satisfied. His imagination runs on with other ways in which the picture could be used, problems it could solve. His smile grows ever broader as he looks towards the artist, but this merely provokes another query.

Snapshot

"Even if you have the place of work, the people and the products, you still only capture the business at a moment in time, a frozen snapshot."

"Yes but we've covered everything. I mean what else can you include?'

Jim strains to make sure every avenue had been explored, tracing out on the table top with his finger, his mind's eye version of the picture as he does so. He offers the artist the product of his somewhat laboured and half-hearted search.

"My great grandfather as the founder I suppose. It would be nice to include him, if we can get agreement."

After straining for a few moments more he reluctantly adds,

"… customers and suppliers, but it starts to get very cluttered, even if we just included their logos, and it would lose the 'old style' picturesque feel of the building."

After a further moment or two of reflection he adds in confirmation, "I think we'd spoil the effect if we have a string of logos across the picture."

Sensing that his response is still seen as deficient, he offers what he sees as a compromise.

"Maybe we can include customer and supplier logos on the back of the Christmas cards and calendar, along with a thank you message."

Warming to his own suggestion as he makes it, he adds, "Yes that's how we deal with those. We'll include them, without it spoiling the overall effect."

It feels like he's played his last card, and a winning one he's sure. It's one that recognises the value he's seen in the artist's questioning, which he duly notes, nodding towards the artist as he concludes, "A good idea, but we'll leave them off the painting."

Completion Jim is now certain that his answer is complete. All angles have now been covered and he feels good. Maybe this hasn't been such a bad journey after all. The centenary is sorted and there's still over a year to go. They'll be stunned on Monday. He'll set it all out in a proposal, what needs doing, an outline timescale with plenty of time to get things done. He'll need some sort of a budget figure of course.

With some difficulty Jim pulls the lid from the small container of milk, which he adds to his drink. A quick stir and now even the coffee tastes good.

The idea now fully formed, Jim's thoughts turn to the practicalities.

"You are available to do this?" Jim asks pointedly, and not wanting to leave space for anything but the affirmative, he quickly presses on.

"What sort of a price would we be looking at? I think we'd need to see some of your other work, just to get the budget cleared, that sort of thing you know. But no, this is a really good idea."

He feels that he's put the answer in a box, tied it with a ribbon and posted it home. However this feeling of closure is not shared by the artist.

"I wasn't thinking of adding more to the picture. In fact I wasn't thinking of this picture at all."

For the first time Jim sees that it's clear that they don't share the same view of this idea at all.

The artist continues, "What you've described is a picture of the business frozen at a point in time."

Jim, unsure of what the artist is driving at, tries to decipher the message, turning the response over in his mind attempting to reconcile the question of how an artist could possibly not like the idea of a picture?'

His mind races as he works to diagnose the problem. Maybe he doesn't want the work, or perhaps they don't have the same taste in art? Just what had he replied when he'd asked him about modern art? He tries feverishly to recall the response, without success. Is that it, he only does modern art? He wants to do some kind of cubist thing where we can't recognise the building or any of the people. The question churns over in his mind as he hears the artist add.

"… rather like a photograph."

"Like a photograph?" Jim echoes with little sign of comprehension as this last phrase has become disconnected in his hearing.

"Yes, a frozen snapshot," repeats the artist.

'A photograph?' Jim toys with the phrase and then his understanding springs into focus. That explains it. He wants the work, but is afraid that he won't get it. He's worried that we'll plump for a photograph rather than the expense of a painting. He breathes an audible sigh of relief at the breakthrough. The problem resolved, Jim quickly seeks to clarify the situation.

"No problem. We're definitely not looking for a photograph. I don't think a photograph would be in keeping with the centenary. We're looking for something special. We've always got to take the money into account of course, but within reason I'm definitely thinking that we want a painting."

'You can tell whether a man is clever by his answers. You can tell whether a man is wise by his questions.'
Naguib Mahfouz

"But you're describing a painting that's rather like a photograph, like the portrait and the landscape that you described earlier."

"Of course, that's the sort of painting I'm thinking of." The fears of some strange cubist interpretation again bubble to the surface in Jim's mind.

"But you capture the business at a point in time. It's sort of frozen."

In his puzzlement, Jim thinks through other possible implications of a picture that's not a painting or a photograph, and not frozen. He turns the thought over in his mind again seeking to resolve it.

"Oh I see! No we wouldn't want that."

He smiles to himself, happy that at last he's deciphered the problem as he explains.

"Oh no we definitely...., well I mean, I've seen some and they're, well a bit embarrassing, and after a few years, well a painting ages so much better."

"Much better than?" It's the artist's turn to be bemused.

"We don't want a video." Jim explains. "I know some companies make videos to give out to staff and even customers, but personally I've always found them a bit, well tacky. I'm definitely thinking painting, paints..., easel..., artist..., the works."

A Painting   He imitates as best he can an artist adding paint to a canvas to underline his point, and seeing this as absolute confirmation of his requirement, feels finally contented that he's now driven the point home. He wonders that so much confusion could surround such a simple requirement, but surely now there can be no doubt that a painting is what he wants. His contentment however is only fleeting.

"No, not a video. That's not what I mean," the artist declares as he now attempts to unravel the confusion.

"Oh I thought with you saying frozen."

"No, the video would still be a point in time, like a film from the twenties, frozen in time even though it shows people moving around. No what I mean is that the painting you've described is a picture of the business, but it *isn't* the business, doesn't get inside what the business is."

Seeing the puzzled expression now draped across Jim's face, and in an attempt to block a number of further blind alleys, the artist quickly adds.

"I don't mean pictures taken inside the business. I mean what the business is, rather than what it does and who does it, and where."

Jim senses that his solution is beginning to drift away. His neatly packaged proposal, the presentation on Monday morning, and the response, the praise, all beginning to slip from his grasp. All teased away by the artist's relentless unwillingness to leave the answer be. He's in no doubt that the artist's questioning has helped create a solution, a good solution that fits his needs. They've solved the problem, solved several problems and it's now time to leave it alone. Why the need to keep challenging it? They have a good solution and the artist has some ready made work. Surely they've explored all the possible alternatives and ruled them out. He can't see how he could make it any clearer that the painting is exactly what he wants.

He buys a little time by picking up his coffee mug and taking an exaggerated time to drink from it. Recognising the opportunity to pause, the artist does the same.

Jim gathers his thoughts and confesses,

Doing

"I think you've lost me. The business _is_ what it does, the people, the factory, the products and services, surely?"

Perhaps there's a hint of frustration showing through in his voice. Valuable though the questions have been, and in spite of the vested interest he feels in the new partnership forged with the artist, the questions are now beginning to jar. He was confident that they'd covered everything. No, he knew for certain that there couldn't be anything else. Of course the artist knows nothing of business, but even so his patience had limits.

'Opinions founded on prejudice are always sustained with the greatest violence.'
Hebrew Proverb

He sensed that now could be a good time to steer the conversation in a new direction, but part of him wanted to hear more of the artist's perspective. If he'd listened to his thoughts more closely, they may have revealed that he looked forward less to hearing the artist's views, and more to engineering the opportunity to express his own. He anticipated the sport of describing the realities of how difficult real business in the real world, and his progress within it, really was. This was a well rehearsed description and one he had used, on occasions, to defend against the ignorance of people who simply didn't understand. However his desire to see through his new centenary solution, made him redouble his efforts to tolerate the artist's questioning and try to resist, for the moment at least, the temptation to set him straight. With a thinly veiled hint of resignation he composed himself to invite the artist to continue, or was it a playful invitation for the artist to stick out his chin so he could deliver his knockout punch?

"You seem to think the picture is something else, so what do you think a painting of our business would be?"

The artist pushed himself back in his seat as he considered the invitation for a moment.

"Well I think your business is about satisfying need of some sort."

'Oh really?' Nothing profound there, Jim thought. Another statement of the obvious. He could have said that about any business, or any organisation for that matter. Not much of a contest swatting that fly.

The artist continued.

Connections

"It's about connections. Maybe I'd see a picture of connections between need and satisfaction."

"Connections?"

'Everything we see is a shadow cast by that which we do not see.'
Martin Luther King, Jr.

Perhaps Jim's modern art alarm had been triggered. He tried to think what a picture of connections might look like, and all that came to mind were blobs and streaks of brightly coloured paint, but the artist pressed on.

"These connections are between the people you've mentioned, the people who work in the company, the suppliers, the customers. All of them have needs that the company tries to satisfy, tries to connect together. Need and satisfaction."

Needs and satisfaction, thought Jim. Sounds like what we call making and selling. Maybe an artist would call them connections, but that's just business. These are the same things he's already described. His patience would permit him to try once more to help the artist understand.

"Yes but that's what I said. I mentioned all of the people, and though I don't like the logo idea for the painting, we can include them on the Christmas card."

He set about spelling out how connections were already covered, jabbing at the table-top as he spoke, as if identifying the components of an already completed painting.

"The building, that's where people connect, that's where they come together. I know we're painting the offices, but that represents them coming together. That's ok isn't it, artistic licence."

He smiles, keen for feedback to confirm that they're now talking of the same thing, and desperate to keep his now clearly brilliant idea alive as he continues.

"And the products are what we connect together to produce. They're the link if you like. We all contribute to the products in one way or another. Whether we make them, supply the bits or just clean up the place afterwards; we all join together; all of us connect through the products."

Recalling the last of the artist's trio of contributors he adds,

'He must be very ignorant for he answers every question he is asked.'
Voltaire

"And the customers, of course they're who we make the connections for. They are what it's all about."

Then as if to explain a supplementary flash of insight he adds, "They're not in the picture, but

47

we're giving the calendar to customers to represent the connection with them."

A moment's reflection allows Jim to see the artist's suggestion in new light.

"Actually, 'connections' isn't such a bad idea. It's a good way of describing the picture. Perhaps that's what we'll call it - 'Connections'.

In his mind's eye he again sees the completed painting. Now it is surrounded by an ornate gilded frame, centred in the bottom of which is a small plaque inscribed with the title. He reads it aloud,

"A Century of Connections."

Jim smiles and adds, confident that it will meet with approval, "That's perfect, and suitably enigmatic and arty."

The artist's smile recognises the effort that Jim has expended in explanation, but his reply remains defiant,

Different   "I think my painting would be different."

Jim's sense of satisfaction is immediately deflated, and for a moment he sits back in his seat a little exasperated. A sip from his coffee serves to excuse his lack of response, and the artist steps in to continue.

"Your painting describes what happens. But it's static, even if it's a picture of people moving, or a process moving, it's still static."

'Things are static when they're moving?' puzzles Jim to himself. No he isn't ready to return to the fray just yet and continues to silently comfort his coffee cup.

"When I think of connections, I think of something dynamic. It's a living thing, something vibrant, that's what makes your business, any business, any organisation; that living vibrancy."

Jim quietly agrees, but the picture he imagines drawn out on the table top already has everything, the building, the people, the products, the services they deliver. That's the living business, everything, all the parts in one picture. He decides to make a further attempt to convince the artist.

"I'm not sure that I know what you mean by dynamic. We have everything in the one picture, it's all there!"

"I agree that the painting represents all of the features of the business," replies the artist, "but there's still something missing. If we think of your painting for a moment."

It's the artist's turn now to point to the nonexistent picture, which rests between them on the table-top, as he continues.

"Well for example, you haven't always had your offices at the same location, and even if you had you won't always be there. One day you're bound to move."

His finger strikes a cross through the imagined office block.

Jim's nod acknowledges what he sees as another statement of the obvious, as the artist continues.

"And certainly in 98 years you've had lots of new people and will continue to have new people. None of us escapes the march of time." He rubs his finger back and forth as if to erase the people from the picture.

"And the products, the products you produce; they might be fine today, but they're a million miles from what you made almost a century ago."

A nod of Jim's head acknowledges more statements of the obvious.

"Even if you're in the same line of business, the materials, design, manufacturing processes will have changed out of all recognition." With a flurry the artist erases the neat arrangement of circled products.

"Yes I know." Jim responds as he hears a catalogue of features, all part of the picture he's already described.

The artist continues, determined not to be deflected. He's now into his stride and keen to shake Jim with the scope of change the business must have faced.

"Maybe you've even switched type of business, perhaps several times during your history. If you hadn't done these things then the business would almost certainly have disappeared. There aren't many business opportunities for people to ride to work on horseback, and operate steam powered machinery to produce products for customers wearing bowler hats and riding bicycles."

Erased

The artist tries to conjure up an image of life a century earlier and raises his hands swaying from side to side in his seat to imitate wobbling along on a penny farthing, before ranging his fingers back and forth across the breadth of the painting, dismissing it in total.

'True Science teaches, above all, to doubt, and to be ignorant.'
Miguel de Unamuno.

Jim smiles and nods at the artist's lack of comprehension as he responds. "The business; it's all in the picture."

He points his hand to direct the artist's gaze towards the table and the hotly contested battleground of Formica, on which he still clearly sees the invisible, but vivid picture of the business as he continues.

"I know it keeps changing. How I wish that it didn't, but in the picture are all of the features of the business. That is the business. You can't rub it all out because it changes, otherwise there's nothing left. There's never going to be anything to paint. It's always changing. In business we just can't stand still."

He resists the temptation to add, 'unlike some piece of the landscape.'

"Precisely," responds the artist. "That's exactly my point. That's why I've rubbed out those parts of the painting, because they keep changing. They are static snapshots, footprints made at a point in time. Footprints made by the business, but they aren't the business."

He chooses to see Jim's total confusion as a signal to continue

"You've had to change and keep changing in those 98 years. That's why you are still in business. Not because you have a head office in a particular place or the people you have today, or the products you currently make or made at any point."

Jim's prepared response to those ignorant of business is now triggered as he feels the anticipated attack on what he has achieved, and the challenges of real business life.

"Oh but hang on a minute. We wouldn't be in business at all without our people, and with no products..." but he is quickly interrupted. The artist is keen to make his point.

"You're right, they are incredibly important, in some ways perhaps more important than you appreciate, but your picture makes them important at a point in time. Your painting captures a point in time, but that isn't the key ingredient of your business, or of your people. What is key is the dynamic, the continuous thread that runs through the business. It's the thread that provides the continuity to allow the business to meet the challenges it has faced over the past 98 years."

Jim, deep in thought of what the comment about 'people being more important than he appreciates' might mean, passes up the opportunity to interject.

"Now those challenges are all history; ninety eight years worth of history. Of course what's important to you now, today, is to ask what is it that is ensuring that your business will meet the challenges it faces today, tomorrow and everyday for the next 98 years?"

"Well that's the same thing, good people and products." Jim offers the same glib answer as before."

The artist's raised eyebrows and a moments silence entice Jim to elaborate.

"It's the business. The business is what makes the business successful, surely?"

As he says it, he feels an inadequacy in the answer and the circularity of the argument, but it's the only answer he has. It is the answer, and he's at a loss as to how else he could describe it.

The artist attempts to frame the difficulty.

"Maybe, but I don't mean the challenges of doing what you do. I mean the challenges of doing what you will need to do."

Designers

"You mean new products?" Jim replies, sure that he has the answer. "We have designers, good designers who are working on the next designs, but they're included in the painting. I included the designers."

He felt sure that he'd made it clear that he'd included all of the people, all departments in the picture; everyone.

"Well the designers might be part of it, but they're just designing for what you know. They're extending a little into the future."

Jim's hears a dismissive tone in the artist's comment, to which he reacts. "But they're our design team. We've got some really clever people. That's what they do!"

He sees yet further proof that the artist doesn't understand the intricacies of business. They had a whole team of people whose main job was to come up with new products and new ideas. What could the artist know of dealing with the future?

"But in 98 years you've seen two world wars and a world that's been totally transformed several times over." The artist searches for an illustration that would extend Jim's thinking. "Take women for example. Your painting will have a fair few women in it?"

"Yes of course."

"And some are in senior positions?" The artist adds

Jim struggles for a moment, not because there are few women, but because there are many. They're not difficult to recall by being rare, but because they are so common and have blended in. Their sex is no longer an issue and he barely recognises it.

He begins to count them out on the raised fingers of his hand. "Yes the marketing manager, northern sales director, head of finance, the personnel director, yes there are lots of women."

"Ninety-eight years ago that probably wouldn't have been the case." offers the artist.

"I guess not." Jim recalls the pictures taken in the twenties of people arriving for work. As he does so he smiles at the comic image, an overriding impression of a sea of hats, bowler hats, trilby hats pouring from works busses and streaming through the ornate front gates of the original factory. He muses on what might have happened to all those hats and the people who made them. But women? Not in the photographs at least.

"If you think of the other kinds of changes that have taken place in that time, the span of a lifetime if we're lucky and eat healthily." adds the artist. "For example, changes in society, what customers expect, what employees expect for that matter."

Sensing that the picture he's painted has been extended sufficiently, he adds, "You didn't look just to your designers to deal with those issues!"

"Designers, no of course not." Jim replies and his thoughts return to his previous answer which, as he repeats it in his mind, feels increasingly inadequate, 'It was the business that dealt with those issues, the business that made the business successful.'

The feeling of inadequacy leads him to add quietly,

"The business…, but what part of the business?"

He scans his mental list, the physical things, buildings, equipment, the products, the people. He can't pinpoint the answer in his picture. He's not sure what this means, but for the first time he senses that it's something different, that there might be something else to describe the business, some other characteristic, some facet that isn't in his picture. Something he's not previously been aware of.

First glimpse   He hasn't a name for it, but he can feel that something must have enabled the business to deal with those changes. He can see that there is a something else, and begins to wonder what it could be.

There's no need for the prompt of being asked what this something is. He has only glimpsed its shadow, but now his mind is intrigued to find out more. He wants to know, and senses that the question he's being asked is now different. No, it's exactly the same question, the difference is that he is now hearing a question. It's no longer a request for knowledge, something known, the retrieval of a piece of information from storage. It's a question. It's about something he doesn't know, something he needs to create.

For the first time Jim begins to see the question, 'What picture would describe your business?' as a question. He'd been answering on autopilot; answers drawn from his catalogue of responses. How do you describe your business? Well bricks, mortar, bodies, work, equipment etc. This was the way he saw the business, the way he understood the business, the way he's always understood the business. This is what he'd understood made the business work.

In truth it's what featured in the plans, the budgets, the discussions, the briefcase full of papers and meeting minutes he had at his feet. Whichever piece of paper he looked at, behind it was an assumption that the business was described by what it did, the premises it

'I prepared excitedly for my departure, as if this journey had a mysterious significance. I had decided to change my mode of life. "'til now," I told myself, 'you have only seen the shadow and been well content with it; now, I am going to lead you into the substance.'
Nikos Kazantzakis.

occupied, the equipment it bought, the people it employed.

He allowed the competing thoughts of how he knew the business was described, and this new sense of incompleteness, to jostle for position in his mind. The current picture, the long standing and previously unchallenged champion, and a newly discovered and unknown upstart.

Support for the champion was overwhelming. It wasn't just he, or his briefcase full of papers, that thought the business was defined in this way, the business also thought it was. He mused for a moment as he glimpsed another circular argument. Everything that describes the business, believes it is defined by the things that describe the business.

Question

The thought was fleeting. He didn't have an answer, but he did now have a question. What was it that made the business? What would you capture in a painting?

'That which has been believed by everyone, always and everywhere, has every chance of being false.'
Paul Valéry

Without knowing at all what it might be, he could now sense that there was an alternative way of picturing the business, what the artist called the dynamic.

"I see." He paused for a moment trying to sense his emergent new understanding. He felt that his circular argument encircled something, but failed to capture this aspect of the business. Like a thrown lasso, seemingly complete in every respect, but failing to ensnare its target.

"The dynamic. It's not those things is it, those things in my painting?"

"That's not what I'd have in mine," the artist confirmed.

The painting had all the parts of the business, they'd agreed that, but didn't describe this feature. It wasn't that he needed to add something to the picture, a piece he'd missed. He'd spent all of his working life in the business; there were no pieces he hadn't seen. What was needed was a new way of seeing, new eyes to see with, not new things to see.

This felt strange. He wasn't sure what this new way was, he couldn't grasp it. Like a name you trawled your memory for, but couldn't quite recall. You felt the shape of the name, the kind of sound it made and your senses knew it was there. You could taste it, but you couldn't speak it. The radiating rings on the surface of the pond, but no sign of the cause of the disturbance.

He didn't want to speak or hear for a moment whilst he concentrated on grasping this thought, making it visible, but try as he could he didn't seem able to. Just like the name stuck on the tip of the tongue, he couldn't bring his new thought into focus. There was no alternative, he would have to ask for more clues.

"What would your picture look like?" he asked the artist.

"I'm not sure that I know."

Jim wasn't prepared for this response. He felt for the first time he'd been persuaded to hesitantly venture from the shallows to the deep, and just as his feet no longer touched the ground, he found the hand he held belonged to someone who swam no better than he did.

As he listened to the artist, it appeared that he too was grappling with tastes that refused to take form. Though the artist couldn't describe the shape, he began to describe the space within which it would fit.

Dynamic "Well what I mean by the dynamic is the ability that let's you deal with changing situations. I'm not thinking of the changes themselves. I don't mean a list of managing directors, or the series of properties you've occupied, or the history of different products."

The artist waved his hand again across the table top, as if to underline the erasure of the now discredited picture.

"Dynamic means the act of changing, rather than the state of being changed or the different states you've passed through."

Not for the first time Jim's puzzled expression served as a prompt for the artist to continue.

"I think this is an important difference. Often when we think of change we think of moving from one position to another, one situation to the next."

"Well yes, that kind of captures the idea." Jim confirmed another apparent statement of the obvious.

"Well, that's not what I mean by the word change. I see that as static. Someone used to be based in Glasgow and then moved to Manchester. It's change, but it's static, the translation from one position to another." Pointing again at the imagined picture on the table top he adds,

"Your painting would simply show two head offices, the old and the new. That's not what I mean by change."

"No?"

"Not at all. I guess we could call that chang-*ed*." The artist placed special emphasis on the ending of the word, before continuing.

"The location was Glasgow and it's now *changed* to Manchester for example, they're nouns. What I mean by the dynamic is the act of changing. The act of moving. The verb."

He takes a sip from his coffee cup and this time choosing to see Jim's puzzled expression as one receptive to finding out more, he presses on, trying to think of an illustration. He sees the now fully unfolded ball of packaging adorning the table top.

Butterfly "Ok, think of the caterpillar. We all know what that becomes."

"The butterfly." Jim replies.

"Yes, we see change as the butterfly in place of the caterpillar, but neither caterpillar nor butterfly is changing."

Jim looks on a little puzzled. "But that's what happens. The caterpillar becomes the butterfly."

"Yes it does, but the action of change is what happens in the chrysalis, the part we easily overlook."

"The chrysalis? I guess so," agrees Jim.

"Of course, the paradox is that the one place where there isn't any movement, is the place where change is taking place."

"Yes you're right, now you mention it I guess it's easy to overlook the chrysalis."

Then, as a recollection comes to mind he adds,

"I mean we learn that at school. A few weeks ago my five year old daughter Jenny brought home pictures of a caterpillar, chrysalis and butterfly she'd painted at school. But you're right, we do think of the caterpillar and the butterfly, and forget where the change actually happens."

He then adds in summary,

"So change isn't movement, and it's not the transformation from one thing to another."

Having said what it wasn't, this seemed to have erased Jim's options for what it was, just as effectively as the artist had erased his table top picture. He struggled for a moment with how to express what remained; what change actually is.

"It's the act of making the change?" he offered.

"Well yes and no." Replied the artist, and fearing that his answer isn't helping, adds,

"I don't mean the process of changing. Things like selecting premises, loading up lorries, carrying equipment from one to the other. I mean the dynamic of being able to change."

The artist feels the frailty of the differentiation between these descriptions, and knows that this frailty will be magnified in Jim's mind.

'As for the future, your task is not to foresee it, but to enable it.'
Antoine de Saint-Exupery

"It's difficult to explain the difference, but it's …"

Then like the frantic act of a child on the beach defending their sandcastle from the returning tide, he throws a string of examples to reinforce the difference.

"…. the ability to sense when change is needed…, the ability to understand the options…, to consider and evaluate them…, the ability to decide and make changes…, the ability to understand what the change was intended to achieve, and assess whether it was successful."

He barely draws breath before throwing yet more examples, "The ability to measure and the ability to learn…, so you know what worked and why, and you know how you might do something even better next time."

Having exhausted his supply of examples, he concludes slightly apologetically, "That's what I mean as the dynamic."

Jim feels that the tide has just swept over him, and takes a few moments to reflect before replying.

"So not moving, but having the ability to move?" he offers as the product of his attempt to gather together the impressions formed from the artist's examples. He's still far from confident that his understanding is secure.

"Yes, I think so. A set of abilities to change, a sort of change-ability. Less concerned with what we do, and more the way we see and think."

"Change-ability?" Jim echoed, acknowledging that this might be the first glimpse of the missing facet of the business he sought. He perhaps had a label, but to what he could attach it, he as yet had little idea.

Tiger The artist continues his description, "That's what I'd try to capture in the painting. It's like, well imagine, a tiger. Imagine a picture of a tiger."

His fingers flash across the table top as he draws out the invisible outline of the animal.

"Let's imagine that I can capture every detail, the colour and texture of the fur, the shape of the mouth, the gleam in its eye. Maybe if I'm very good I even succeed through its facial expression in capturing the thoughts in its head. Even if I'm that good, do I capture any more than what a taxidermist can capture? The stuffed head on a wall, or the tiger displayed in a glass case in a museum?"

Jim ponders for a moment the idea of a stuffed tiger's head.

'The purpose of art is to lay bare the questions which have been hidden by the answers.'
James Arthur Baldwin

"I'm not sure what thoughts there would be in the tiger's head mounted on the wall, but I see what you mean. But you have drawn the tiger."

"Yes but…" The artist presses on, seeing the opportunity to cement his point. "… If an alien came down to Earth and wanted to know about tigers, I've captured what it looks like, but I haven't captured what it is, what it is to be a tiger. That's what I'd want to capture in your painting. Not what you do, but who you are. Not what you've done, but how you can go on to achieve."

Jim tentatively offered his newly formed understanding, recognising that it was largely a guess.

"So the dynamic isn't what we're doing, it's what we're going to do?"

Being not doing "Nearly. It's not what you're doing, or have done, or even what you will do. In fact it's not at all what you do. It's what you are, what you are being and what you are capable of becoming."

Despite the artist's encouragement, it didn't feel to Jim that his guess had been near at all. What little understanding he thought he'd had, seemed to evaporate. The word that was just about to be retrieved from the tip of his tongue, had slipped from his grasp again.

Sensing this, the artist continued.

"I think that a painting of your great grandfather would be a poor one if it only told me his height and looks, what he wore, the arrangement of his features, or even if it told me what he did.

I'd want a painting that told me what he was, and what it was about him that would create a business that would still be successful 98 years later, long after he has passed on. A picture of what he was capable of becoming."

"But you said you didn't want a painting of what he did," replied Jim

"That's right, but what he was, and what he did, are two quite different things."

In an attempt to help clarify the difference he added,

"Think of the difference as what he was being, rather than what he was doing. You see?"

Jim response confirmed that he didn't really see at all. "Being and doing? Well he was being a founder of the company, and what he was doing was founding the company. They feel like the same thing."

'Any great work of art revives and readapts time and space, and the measure of its success is the extent to which it makes you an inhabitant of that world -- the extent to which it invites you in and lets you breathe its strange, special air.'
Leonard Bernstein

"That's only because you're letting them be the same," The artist responded. "It's what we mostly do. People ask who you are, and we answer as if they've asked what we do; schoolteacher, businessman, or artist I guess. But there is a difference, if we let there be one. For the moment just allow the idea of a difference, even if you don't see one." He nods towards Jim and adds, "Can you sense a gap?"

"Ok. I'm trying." Jim was far from sure what a gap might look like, let alone whether he could see one.

The artist tried to help, "Well imagine a picture of a schoolteacher, stood in their gown. That's what the person is currently doing, but it might not be what they were doing yesterday.

Perhaps yesterday they were driving a lorry, and perhaps tomorrow they will be fighting fires."

"But they've just changed from being a lorry driver, to being a teacher, to being a fireman."

"Yes that's what you'll see if you don't allow the gap," confirmed the artist. "But try to think of a difference between doing and being."

"I am trying." replied Jim, who was trying, in that way you do when determined to help carry a piano, but unsure as to whether you should push or pull.

"So, do you know anyone who has had those three jobs, lorry driver, teacher, fireman?" asked the artist.

After the briefest thought Jim replied, "Well, no, of course not."

"Nor me. It seems like quite a combination, quite a difficult thing, to be qualified to do all three. I guess that there aren't many who have, or many who could have those three jobs.

He pauses for a moment before adding,

"So someone who did, might be a little bit special?"

"I guess so," Jim agrees.

"So there is something about that person that enables them to do those three jobs, something that allows the connection."

There's that word 'connections' again thought Jim, and his mind begins to stir as the artist continues.

"They haven't simply done those three things, appeared in those three snapshots. There is something else, something they are being that makes them the kind of person who could be a lorry driver, a teacher and a fireman."

The stirring takes effect, and Jim replies,

"I see what you mean. Connections, yes something that connects. Of course not every teacher can be a fireman, maybe some could be something else, make some other connections in what they're being."

Future

As the gap opened up and he sensed the separation between doing and being, he thought of his great grandfather. The pictures he'd seen of him taken in the twenties when the business was already successful, flashed across his mind. He'd sometimes looked at those pictures. The family resemblance was clear. They were connected in how they looked. Were they also connected by what they were?

Echoes of past conversations of family characteristics and resemblances drifted through his mind. And then he was struck by a new question. Could the picture reveal what his great grandfather was capable of becoming? Could the picture taken in the twenties have captured something about his great grandfather's future, and a picture of the business, captured its future also? His mind whirred with the possibilities.

"So the dynamic is the ability to change, the connection?"

"Yes exactly", confirmed the artist increasingly confident that these words described a shared understanding.

Jim continued to think of the photographs of his great grandfather stood in his finest business clothes. Standing almost at attention, he looked towards the camera, smiling behind his large white moustache and projecting confidence. A chain led to his top pocket which Jim assumed held his gold pocket watch. His hands clasped in front of his waist were almost hidden under the hat he was holding. 'Yet another hat', Jim thought.

Jim recognised that he always became acutely conscious of his own hands when being photographed. Most of the time they just sat there at the end of his arms doing what came naturally. But as soon as a camera appeared, what were you meant to do with them? Hold them behind you, thrust into pockets or clasped in front. Maybe this was his great grandfather's answer, hide them by holding your hat.

The picture captured his stature, and reflected a point in time, but where in this picture was his great grandfather's ability to change? In contemplating the question, he struggled to imagine what signs, what evidence he was even looking for. But one clue now came into focus and could be described.

"So change is an ability, not an activity."

"I like that. Yes exactly," agreed the artist with a smile.

'A work of art does not answer questions, it provokes them; and its essential meaning is in the tension between the contradictory answers.'
Leonard Bernstein

"And you'd paint a picture of this ability? Not what we've changed, but how we were able to change." asked Jim

"Well not how you *were* able to, but how you *are* able to change. Your change-ability."

For the moment Jim fails to hear the distinction between these two phrases. In his mind's eye he visualises a painting, that by some means reveals how the business was able to deal with change, and is fascinated by the idea.

"That's what you'd paint?" asks Jim after rolling the idea around in his head for a few moments to feel its shape.

"That's the painting I'd like to see. I don't know that I could paint it, but that's what I'd be looking for."

Jim still had the images of his great grandfather in mind. Those pictures captured all the things the artist had said made it a poor picture of change-ability, his stature, dress and looks. But a picture of what he was, what he was capable of becoming! He begins to imagine the value of such a picture.

Then the significance dawns on him, "I see."

"What?" asks the artist.

What you said a moment ago." He echoes the phrase used by the artist, "How you are able to change." and begins to recognise its significance. "When you said it was a picture of how you *are* able to change. The picture is created before the change, but captures the ability to change."

He adds slowly as the realisation fully dawns, "… to change in the future?"

The significance of this distinction wraps its arms around him as he gives voice to his understanding.

Crystal Ball   "Well of course any change must be in the future. If the picture taken in the twenties reveals the future that the company had ahead of it, my great grandfather could have looked at that picture, and seen into the future."

He then adds what suddenly becomes a growingly obvious question.

"Maybe even being able to change things to make the future better?"

"That's the real magic," adds the artist. "It's a picture of what the future holds."

Jim contemplates this picture of the future before asking, "A sort of crystal ball?"

Shaking his head the artist replies, "It's not a picture of what will happen,"

"But…"

"It's a picture of the future none the less," the artist continues. "A picture of the ability to make change happen."

Pointing to the table top he sketches a new picture frame with his fingers as he adds, "A picture of how well you will address what happens, and what needs to happen."

"But if it's a picture of the future? Isn't that what's going to happen?" Jim asks.

"The future isn't a place where you can know what's going to happen, – that's impossible. The picture tells you what's capable of happening. Chance, circumstance, good and bad fortune and a thousand other things will also be part of the future. The painting isn't a guarantee. In fact it's the opposite of that. As soon as you see it as a guarantee, then it's bound not to be."

"I guess so?" Jim adds with so complete an absence of conviction that it serves to prompt the artist to explain.

"If you think the future is assured, you stop working for it and destroy the very things that would create it. No, the picture tells you what's capable of happening. Create a picture with lots of capability, and on balance great things are going to happen. You can't know how and where in advance, or exactly what they will be, but they're going to happen."

"So it's the future. But not the detail?"

"You can't have a detailed picture of the future. If you did, the very fact that you knew it, would change it."

"But?"

"Well imagine you know you're going to win the Olympic gold medal. Once you know, then what's the point in training? You know it's bound to happen, so why go through the pain of getting up at four in the morning, running 25 miles and lifting weights seven days a week, when you could be having fun and still win. All you need do is turn up and run and collect the medal."

"And you don't train so you don't win," surmises Jim.

"Precisely. Knowing the future is quite different to that. It's knowing that you are going to win the gold medal, not instead of the training but because of it. Because of the change-ability, that you are building up."

"So you don't know, I mean for sure, that you are going to win the gold medal."

'Winners have the ability to step back from the canvas of their lives like an artist gaining perspective. They make their lives a work of art -- an individual masterpiece.'
Denis Waitley

"Oh you do. And it's for sure." the artist responds animatedly. "Really wanting to win, is how you become the winner. You are being the winner, before it happens. That's what gives you the power and leads to you winning."

Sensing Jim's quizzical expression, the artist adds. "The problem is that most people don't really want to be winners."

"What do you mean? They want to loose?"

"No. It's not that they want to lose. They like the idea of winning but they don't want to *become*, a winner."

"What do they want then?"

"I think they want something to do. They want to do the things to win, but they don't want to become, be, a winner. Their need for a guarantee of success is what prevents them succeeding. Just like the existence of a guarantee of winning means you won't."

"But how?"

Guarantees

'Take the risk of winning.'
Frank Dick

"Because your search for a guarantee means you won't have the energy and will to succeed. It's like people who want to lose weight. Instead of changing what they are being, they want to stay the same, just magically weigh thirty pounds less. They want a guarantee of the end point, but don't want to be what they need to be to get there. They spend their time searching for guarantees, magic diets or pills, then moaning that they didn't work, before they begin to search for the next."

Jim prods absentmindedly at the plastic centrepiece of packaging before speaking.

"I see. It's like they want the static, without the dynamic. To become the butterfly, without the work of the chrysalis."

"Exactly." And building on the same imagery the artist adds, "And what they become is a caterpillar that tries to attach wings to its back. However hard they try, they are never going to fly. The future isn't fixed. Instead of looking for guarantees, they should be building them."

"So change-ability, it's a picture of the future, the ability to change. The ability to win at change in the future."

'Inventing the future requires giving up control. No one with a compelling purpose and a great vision knows how it will be achieved. One has to be willing to follow an unknown path, allowing the road to take you where it will. Surprise, serendipity, uncertainty and the unexpected are guaranteed on the way to the future.' George Land.

Jim muses, his mind starting to race with the thought of what that picture could do. A picture that could tell his grandfather in 1920, how the business would be able to succeed through a future in which he couldn't have known what would happen, couldn't even have guessed at it, but could know how well his business would deal with that future. Magic was a good word for this. He began to test what this magic might mean.

"In nineteen-twenty my great grandfather couldn't have known the Second World War was only nineteen years away"

"No, for sure. The first world war had only ended two years earlier."

"But he could know how well he would deal with it when it came?"

"I think so," the artist confirmed, and watched as Jim rolled the answer around in his mind, savouring the power of the idea.

Excitedly Jim asked, "I'm not sure what that picture would look like?"

"Nor me."

That was not the answer Jim had set himself to hear. His feet felt to be even further from the comforting ground of the shallows. He'd sensed the unease of questions that questioned, and to this was added the discomfort of admitting to having no answers. He felt that this was the time for the artist to provide an answer, a definition, and yet he gave none.

'A business's flexibility in adapting to change and market dynamics will mark the winners and losers in this fast-changing internet age.' Michael Dell

Jim had been drawn into seeing a new way of describing their business. Connections; a picture of connections the artist had said. He felt the need to make connections himself. He was now intrigued by what this picture might look like, but more intrigued by a sense that it connected with a need he felt. He wanted the artist to reveal more and tried to tease it from him.

"But if you were able to paint it, to paint our ability to change, that would be a valuable picture."

Jim senses connections to be made, but can't yet describe them. He sets out to state this new understanding, as if to strengthen the imprint in his thinking.

"I see what you mean about the dynamic and the static. It's not a picture of a point in time, or points in time, it's a picture of movement, no, the ability to move, to change. A picture of what the business is, not what it does."

But just as he thinks he has the thought in focus, it begins to slip away.

He runs through the discussion in his head and the mass of evidence that contradicts this new thought, and continues to point to a picture of what the business does. It's not just the briefcase full of papers, but the body of meetings they represent, the people at those meetings, and the people they work for or have work for them. They all have a picture of what the business does. He's seen that picture for thirty years, and what is more, been respected for his knowledge of it. In truth he's progressed because of it, and now he is being tempted to agree that he's never seen, in all that time, what makes the business successful.

What we do The paperwork filling his briefcase reflects the budgets and plans, manpower forecasts, staff appraisals, orders for materials and equipment. The business is about doing. Converting materials into products and delivering services.

The business exists through what it does; 'we are what we do, aren't we?'

He feels himself drawn to his original picture; the totality of the business described in bricks and mortar, people and products and what we do, turning this picture over in his mind. And even if 'what we are' could be painted, what picture would it be? A picture of our change-ability? Even the artist doesn't seem to know what this would be.

'Man's mind, once stretched by a new idea, never regains it's original dimensions.'
Oliver Wendell Holmes

The words echoed in his mind. He was alarmed and intrigued that a picture could exist, an important picture that he'd never seen before. Of course he could deny it or dismiss it, but he felt drawn to learn more. It wasn't simply to keep alive the centenary idea now. He wanted to know what this picture would be, the power it could hold.

His mind raced as he tried to imagine the form the picture could take. Momentarily he recalled the artist's dissection of his initial thoughts, the total erasure of his painting, and as if recognising the validity of its destruction for the first time, expresses his new understanding of the alarming conclusion. "What if the picture was a blank canvas?"

'To really ask is to open the door to the whirlwind. The answer may annihilate the question and the questioner.'
Anne Rice

"What do you mean?" replied the artist clearly intrigued by this new direction.

"Well imagine we didn't have any ability to change; I know that we've got the design team, but imagine if that's all you could paint."

"What, nothing else?"

"That's right. The design team, looking at new products, but nothing else, no other change-ability."

"It might be a scary picture!" offers the artist.

The scary nature of the picture was not lost on Jim, and he sensed how attractive the idea of ignoring it could be. But the thought of this new painting has connected with another fear he has felt, which he now understands and shares with the artist.

"Imagine you'd been able to paint pictures of our competitors, and they'd had a blank painting, no ability to change.

"Go on," nudged the artist.

"Well, don't you see? Maybe they were doing well at the time, good sales, profits ok, things looking up, doing good things, but a blank canvas, and they never even knew."

"I see."

"They'd have a brilliant picture of what they did, bricks, mortar, people, products, profits all

'You are the person who has to decide. Whether you'll do it or toss it aside; You are the person who makes up your mind. Whether you'll lead or will linger behind. Whether you'll try for the goal that's afar. Or just be contented to stay where you are.'
Edgar A. Guest

that stuff, the picture I drew, but their change-ability was just a blank canvas?"

Jim was replaying in his mind's eye what often seemed the fickle process by which companies succeeded or failed. It appeared to him to be a process of chance, where even some of the best performers would suddenly disappear. He recalled conversations with colleagues from competing companies. He'd be speaking to them one day and they'd show not a hint of impending disaster. Of course they talked and shared stories of how things were, things going well and not so well, but that was routine. They wouldn't mention anything really serious, and yet within a couple of months, sometimes sooner, their company would be in crisis and then disappear.

At first he had thought they must have known and were keeping things to themselves. However after several similar experiences, even to people he knew well, he had to conclude that they were simply overtaken by events, things just spiralling out of control.

Deep down that's what worried him the most, being overtaken by events. Facing a challenge head on was one thing, but he feared that they had fallen to something that didn't approach head on, it caught them unawares. It was as if they were swimming on calm water, and then a shark appeared out of nowhere and gobbled them up. That was what frightened him the most about the business. He mulled over the thought of how competitors had fallen to this kind of shark attack, and then suddenly saw it and blurted out,

"It's like, what is it, the film? The film where the picture is in the attic?"

"What, what do you mean?" replied the artist, a little nonplussed.

"The film where he doesn't grow old; he stays young but he has a picture in the attic, a portrait. You must know it. It's a film about a painting."

Jim allowed no room for any possibility that the artist, of all people, would not know the details of a film about a portrait.

The artist after a little thought obliged.

Attic picture "Dorian Grey. The picture of Dorian Grey."

"That's it!"

Jim excitedly outlines the plot as he remembers it.

"The picture is in the attic and the face in the picture keeps getting older and older, but the person, Dorian Grey doesn't. He carries on being young, everything is fine, no problems, but the picture reflects the reality; hidden from sight, but the reality."

Jim is gripped by the parallels he senses with the picture of change-ability.

"Imagine if companies had a picture in their attic that they didn't even know about, that was getting older and weaker, but they couldn't see or sense any of it. To them it felt that things were just fine. No problems at all with what they were doing and nothing to warn them. But in the attic is this picture of their ability to deal with change, an ability they don't even recognise, and it's just fading away."

For a few moments his recollection of the film, tinged with his experience of businesses he'd seen fail, filled Jim's imagination before he continued.

"Maybe they had a powerful founder, like my great grandfather, who did things to set the business on its course. People could see what he did, what the company did, they could paint a picture of that, but no one could see what they were being. No one could recognise or paint that picture of their change-ability. And then he's gone, but the business carries on. They all work hard, very hard, long hours doing the very best they can, doing the things they think matter, doing the things in the painting of what to do.

'All nature is but art unknown to thee;
All chance, direction, which thou canst not see;
All discord, harmony not understood;
All partial evil, universal good;
And spite of pride, in erring reason's spite,
One truth is clear, whatever is, is right.'
Alexander Pope

And it seems to work until one day something changes and just wipes it out."

He let's out an involuntary sigh before adding,

"That's the really scary thing about this business, well not just this business."

"What's that?"

"Well what I said about our competitors all doing the same kind of things."

"Yes"

"Well some of them you could tell, well you could tell that they weren't going to last. But surprisingly they are the exception, and even some of those that I thought were doomed have kept going. The really surprising thing is that in the main, the ones that have gone, I often thought they were better than us. Better products, slicker sales force, more profitable, bigger perhaps…."

"Better …?"

"That's what makes it so hard, so difficult." Jim continued. "You never really know when it's going to be your turn. That's what gives you the sleepless nights."

"And the Saturday morning work…?"

"Yes, that and Sunday's too. You can never feel that you've done enough, because you don't really know when enough has been done. You don't know exactly what needs doing to make sure that it's not your turn this month to be eaten by the shark."

"The shark? So you find yourself doing a bit more?"

"Yes a bit more. Often it must be a waste of time."

Reacting to the artist's look of surprise Jim adds,

"I mean you do things that don't get used, prepare reports that don't get read, go to meetings and wonder why you bothered, agonise for days over decisions that then aren't acted upon, but you feel you have to."

'It is no use saying, 'We are doing our best.' You have got to succeed in doing what is necessary.' Sir Winston Churchill

"To try and make sure?"

"Well that, and for your conscience. I mean if it does happen, if we do go down, then I wouldn't want to think I hadn't tried my hardest."

"Even if you were trying your hardest in the wrong direction?" asks the artist.

"I guess so. Dying with my boots on so to speak"

"Very graphic!"

Jim pauses to reflect for a moment before adding, "But that's the problem. You try to do your best. Try to keep things going, or to make them better, but its all part of the picture I drew. And that's not what's important is it?

"The picture you drew was of what you do. That's the picture that we are most familiar with. For most people it's the only one they ever see, the only one they've ever been aware of. But it's not the only picture. In a changing world what you do is continuously erased by change."

"Just like you erased my picture." Jims hand flashes across the table top, as if to remove any last vestiges of the original.

"That's right. What you do has to be redrawn to reflect change, but even as you redraw it, it's changing again, and again."

"So you can't draw anything."

"Well if what you do isn't changing, it's not worth drawing, it's just a relic of history. If it is changing, then I guess it's just a blur of one thing becoming the next as its constantly redrawn."

He allows a moment for Jim to consider the resulting invalidity of the picture he had previously thought represented the business, and then adds.

"But if you think of how it gets redrawn, how it moves from one to the next."

"Then you are thinking about the dynamic." offers Jim.

"That's right."

No movement "The chrysalis that doesn't move, but is the ability to change. So there are two paintings. What we do, and how we change?"

"Yes. What you do, and what you are being." concludes the artist.

For the first time Jim feels he fully grasps the idea of picturing the business, and as he does his sense of achievement is nullified by the realisation that his previous understanding has been thoroughly swept aside. His knowledge, abilities and position all founded on a picture of what the business does, a picture swept aside by the artist.

There's suddenly a prevailing air of melancholy that the artist wants to dispel for fear that it dissipates their thinking. He prompts Jim by asking, "And change-ability is important for your business?"

Jim hears another statement of the obvious, but it serves to rekindle his thoughts.

"Well yes. I mean if everything was static, then there'd be nothing to worry about."

He smiles at the idea, before adding,

"Whatever we earned this week we'd earn next week. Whatever we produced and sold, we'd produce and sell over and again, always for the same price and the same profit."

He adds with a chuckle,

"As long as the world stopped changing on a good week, we'd be absolutely fine."

"A picture of you sort of frozen whilst winning that gold medal!" offers the artist in summary.

"Yes exactly."

Jim thought for a while before adding.

"That's not such a bad analogy either. It's the sort of thing we try and do.

"How so?"

"Well when things go well, we kind of hold our breath; stand like statues. It's like we don't want to touch anything for fear that we break the magic spell. Of course it never lasts.

Customers are always changing. We have problems with machinery. People go off sick or on holiday. Or maybe we just don't know what it was that we did to make things good in the first place."

It's the artist's turn to prod at the unfurled arrangement of packaging as he considers Jim's description.

Freeze   "Maybe trying to keep still and hold your breath is what makes it go wrong," suggests the artist.

"Sorry?" The shift in idea catches Jim unawares.

"Well you said you try to keep things the same, but when you were successful the week earlier, you weren't trying to keep things the same. In fact you must have changed something to make things better than before."

It takes a moment for the significance to register.

"Oh yes, I see what you mean. Absolutely! The act of keeping things the same, isn't the same as what we did for success. Absolutely."

This strikes Jim as a hammer blow the reverberations of which appear as echoes as he repeats to himself what he's discovered.

"Our act of trying to keep ourselves performing well, itself destroys our ability to perform well. I hadn't thought about it that way before, but you're absolutely right."

He re-runs through the thought once more as if with each repeat he unwraps another layer that has been concealing it from view.

"The very act of trying to ensure our success, condemns us to fail. Now that might explain a lot."

He smiles at the paradox, but the smile has a hard edge as he thinks through the consequences of this realisation. Then he adds quietly and with a hint of resignation,

"That's the whole basis for our approach to managing the business and making us competitive."

'Life is a series of collisions with the future; it is not the sum of what we have been, but what we yearn to be.'
Jose Ortega y Gasset

"Eh?"

"Our whole approach is based on trying to capture something good we do and holding on to it. Whether it's something we've done, or something we've seen elsewhere, we think the answer is to apply it, to do it." He idly spins the clump of plastic packaging that sits between them. As it comes to rest he adds.

"I see now that although we think we're moving, we're just like those figures on the old movie film. We are actually frozen, frozen at a point in time. In fact it's worse than that, we seek to freeze ourselves."

The artist remains quiet. It's as if he's watching a huge ice shelf as it reaches into the open water. Cracks are appearing, slowly, almost imperceptibly, but large pieces of ice that once felt to be permanence itself, are falling away, tumbling and crashing into the sea.

"What we were doing, are doing, isn't important is it?"

Without hesitating Jim goes on to answer his own question.

"In a way it's not what we were doing that we needed to capture and hold on to, it's what we were being."

"I think so," the artist nods in agreement.

Jim peers into his coffee cup at what remains of his drink, now cooled and with the crazed pattern of milk fat on its surface, reminiscent of broken ice. He stirs the contents as if trying to inject some semblance of life back in to it. Watching its swirling progress, he adds,

"The dynamic of being able to deal with change, with all the changes that we face, that's what made us perform well for ninety-eight years, that's our secret ingredient?"

Still peering into the swirling contents of his cup, he repeats,

"Yes, I think that's the secret ingredient you were asking about."

He looks up now from the coffee to look directly at the artist as he reveals,

"Now that's really interesting and scary."

"Why's that?"

"Well I like this idea of the dynamic. I hadn't really seen things that way before, didn't know there was that way of seeing. That's not how we look at our business."

'It's not so much that we're afraid of change or so in love with the old ways, but it's that place in between that we fear . . . . It's like being between trapezes. It's Linus when his blanket is in the dryer. There's nothing to hold on to.'
Marilyn Ferguson

He points to the table top, the former home of the now totally discredited picture.

"I thought that the business was the bricks and mortar, people etcetera. I know in a way that it is, but this dynamic is different. Perhaps it's the real key, what makes the business the business. But what's really scary is that we don't just see the business in this static way, we look at change in exactly the same way. We actually see change as kind of static. Just as you said, we see

it as movement from one position to another;
the caterpillar to the butterfly."

The artist's nod offers a barely needed
prompt for Jim to continue,

"Well, having had this conversation, it now
seems bizarre to think of change in that way, it's
a kind of change without changing, being moved
without the act of movement."

The artist nods to encourage him to continue.

"But that's just exactly how we see change.
Well we sort of know that change is happening
all the time. We sort of know it, but we sort of
don't accept it. That is, I mean we behave as if
change only comes along once in a while. I hope
this makes sense…?" Jim wasn't sure that even
he had clear sight of his line of thinking, but the
artist seemed to understand.

"Go on."

"It's a kind of,"

He hesitates in order to collect his thoughts.

"The best way I can describe it is as split
personality. We behave as if everything is the
same, and going to be the same from week to
week, month to month. Now by that I don't
mean identical, we know for example that March
will be busier than January each year, so we

recognise fluctuations, but even these we build in to be the same. Each March will be busier than each January. So we deal with change by building our plans around this static picture."

Jim smiles to himself that he has an increasingly clear picture in his mind of change seen in quite distinctly different ways, as static and dynamic, a picture he hadn't even glimpsed an hour earlier. Almost unwittingly he finds himself keen to expose the ramifications of this new thinking.

Planning "Now we know things will go wrong, say breakdowns, and things might not happen, say orders we don't win, or maybe we win extra orders and we build these as what we call contingency. So we might put some money to one side to buy new equipment or to pay overtime for example. But again these are sort of static. They are lumps of things set to one side to be used at points in time. We carry on with our plan; a static picture of what's going to happen. Oh we meet regularly to discuss the plan, to decide on changes, to shift things, mainly backwards to allow more time for problems we've encountered, but occasionally forwards if things have gone well."

Jim pauses as he visualises a picture of the process in his head.

"And ...?" The artist prompts Jim to continue.

"Do you want to know something?" Jim says as if offering a glimpse into an innermost secret.

Raised eyebrows signal Jim to proceed.

"We even call our plans 'live'. Live because we keep changing them, but they're not live at all, they're not what you and I are calling dynamic."

His new found understanding feels like the sharp edge of a knife that has been able to create two quite distinct parts, static and dynamic, from what was previously a homogeneous blob that barely warranted a moment's consideration. He continues to describe the results of this dissection.

"The plans are static. We follow them sort of ignoring change, unless it builds up to a critical level to catch our attention."

"What do you mean?" asked the artist.

"Well we ignore small signs of change, things that hint at what is happening, and wait for things to come off the rails before we decide to do something about them."

"For example?"

"Well take a simple one; machine breakdowns. Whenever one of these happens it has a big impact on the factory. We get people together quickly to try and sort out where the problem is, which piece of equipment, what's happened, what we need to do to fix it. Perhaps getting outside contractors in for example. We discuss what 'work-arounds' to do."

"Work-arounds?"

"If the equipment is part of a process, we can't stop the whole factory from working whilst we get it fixed, so we look at ways in which we can keep going until things are back to normal."

Sensing the need for an illustration he adds,

"Imagine, well imagine this train breaking down, difficult I know."

They share a smile.

"Well a work around might be a bus service between stations to move passengers past some broken track."

"I see."

"So we do all this, in fact we do this very well, but we never have the time to stop it happening again. Oh I mean we get the equipment fixed properly, and serviced so it's not the same breakdown next time, but sure as you like, another breakdown somewhere else will come along within a few weeks and we do the same all over again."

"Well perhaps things are inevitably going to break?" offers the artist as explanation.

"But that's it. We sit around waiting for them to break."

The act of vocalising problems seems to Jim to have given them a new stark reality. The artist peers out of the window leaving Jim a few moments for thought.

It is the artist who breaks the silence.

Needs

"Well, maybe your people need things to break?"

"Need things to break?" Jim's train of thought is broken by the incongruity of the suggestion.

The future is an opaque mirror. Anyone who tries to look into it sees nothing but the dim outlines of an old and worried face.'
Jim Bishop.

"Of course not," he replies tersely, momentarily seeing the artist again as an unknowing outsider. "It causes massive problems and cost's us a fortune."

The artist bides his time before explaining,

"Just because people curse, doesn't mean they don't welcome it. Maybe they like fixing things. If you fix things you become the centre of attention. There aren't many heroes who just keep things well oiled."

Jim recoils as the artist's softly spoken words have transformed the absurd into the obvious before his eyes. He confesses.

"I think we do,"

As his comprehension of the idea forms, he adds,

"And to fix things you have to make sure that something breaks first!"

The reflex defence of absurdity removed, Jim sees another rational explanation,

"Or maybe we only know what to do when something has broken."

"Yes, that's another good reason to like things to break. It's a really good way of telling what to do next. No need for debates or discussions about priorities. No real thinking either. Just roll up your sleeves and get on with it."

The accusation of not thinking would have previously triggered Jim's defence of the business, but not now.

"Oh we do plenty of thinking in solving problems, or plenty of what we call thinking, but you're right, it's not real thinking. We don't have time to think about the problem, we've only the time to fix it. And that's why it comes back time and again, in different guises, but time and again. We have breakdowns because we need them."

Suddenly they break into spontaneous laughter at a shared revelation. "This train?" they chorus.

"This train has broken down because it needs to. The train company need it to breakdown," reveals Jim.

"They had no idea how they would spend tonight until now, and now they do," echoes the artist.

Jim reflected on his recent travelling experience. Far from an infrequent act of chance, the journeys seemed bedevilled with problems. If it wasn't the train it was the track, or the signalling. When the train ran on time the heating wouldn't work, or when it did, there was no hot water for the coffee. The more he thought about it, the more it seemed to describe both the train company and his own. It wasn't about what they did. It didn't matter how many things they fixed. What caused the problems was what they were, what they were being. That's what needed changing.

Negatives

Jim turns to the Artist as his reflection uncovers a disturbing insight. "Maybe we don't have a blank canvas at all."

"The painting?"

"Maybe the canvas also has on it things that damage our change-ability. The fact that we need to let things break so we can fix them, needs to be painted in there."

The idea that the painting can describe the negative, the absence of a capability, or even the presence of a disability for change, adds a new dimension that Jim needs a moment to consider.

The carriage lurches forwards taking them both by surprise, briefly jolting life into the residue of the two now cold coffee cups. The train moves forwards tentatively as if unsure of what lies ahead, but it is movement. They each scan the windows trying to look into the darkness outside, but see only their own reflections. The artist is the first to pick up the description of negative change-ability.

"I guess so, but you don't just change things to fix them after they've broken. You talked about new technologies and methods. You've recognised that change is important, that it's important to keep up with what's happening."

'The future is not a result of choices among alternative paths offered by the present, but a place that is created-- created first in the mind and will, created next in activity. The future is not some place we are going to, but one we are creating. The paths are not to be found, but made, and the activity of making them, changes both the maker and the destination.'
John Schaar.

103

"Yes, and I thought we were addressing it," replied Jim, "but now I'm not sure that we even understand what change is. We have a change team, and we meet to discuss change, you know plans, things we need to do to improve, but it all feels static. We schedule the meetings, well for a start that kind of feels static."

"Well?"

"We've got change happening all around us and we schedule meetings to discuss it."

"I guess it has to be in diaries," the artist suggests.

"But again it kind of feels like killing it before we've started. Once you think about the dynamic, everything starts to look frighteningly static. Anyway we schedule meetings and people put in suggestions, we discuss them and make decisions."

"Decisions? That doesn't quite feel like the end of the process," queries the artist.

"Well no, I guess not. Sometimes it is though. We decide something and, well maybe we get sidetracked and that's as far as it goes, sadly." Jim is momentarily distracted as he recalls the effort put into proposing change and agreeing it, only for nothing to happen. He wonders how much of what he has in his briefcase will really matter, how much will make a difference.

"But not always?" offers the artist.

"Sorry." Jim replies as he is disturbed from his thoughts.

"That's not always the end point."

"No sometimes we do apply the decision, we do something with it, put the idea into action."

"What sort of ideas?"

"Well they can be anything, from anyone really. Some come from our workers, some from customers, it depends. Sometimes we might have seen something a competitor is doing for example."

He thinks of example ideas as he continues,

"They have to be inexpensive, we seem to weed out things that will cost money, but some do get through."

"They lead to a change?"

PDCI   "Some of them, yes." Then as if triggered by the word change and truly making the connection for the first time he adds,

"You'll be impressed by this. We sometimes use a change process. I think the Chairman had seen it somewhere so he suggested it, and well we try to humour him. Now what's it called, PCDI, Plan...., Do, no that's it PDCI, Plan, Do, Check, Improve. It's a way of making changes. The way he explained it, it was just simple common sense."

Leaning forward in his seat the artist asks, "And you humour him?"

"Well yes. It made sense when he explained it, but in reality we've not really found it very useful. I mean it is quite simple. You have a plan for what you intend to do, you do the things in the plan, you check if it's worked, and you find things you could improve so that it can work better next time."

"Well it sounds simple enough. And you say you haven't managed to get it to work? On the face of it, that seems quite an achievement."

"What?"

"Well getting something so simple not to work. A bit like getting a train not to run between two points." adds the artist.

"Shush, don't let the train hear you." Jim whispers.

Though progress is slow, the train is still moving forwards, and Jim doesn't want them to tempt fate.

The artist continues,

Plan to Paint "Ok so let's imagine that I'm going to do a painting using this process. What happens?"

"I'm not sure you can fit this process to creating a painting."

"That's ok. Let's give it a try," replies the artist.

"Well you start with a plan; you're going to paint a landscape for example."

"Ok a landscape." The hint of resignation in the artist's response speaks of his disappointment at the choice of example.

"In the plan you'd have the idea for the painting; you have the equipment, the paints, easel; and resources, the place and time to paint it for example."

"Ok, so that's the plan step, then I 'do' the painting. I sit and paint?"

"Yes that's right, the do part is the main part of the process," Jim confirms.

"Then I check. What's that?"

'The greatest
inventions and
accomplishments
began as the flicker of
an idea. This tiny
flame then fuelled by
desire and faith.
Watch out for those
tiny ideas. You have
the potential to turn
them into great
things.'
Steve Brunkhorst

"Well that's where you compare the picture to the scene, the one you are trying to paint. Note the good things and the bad."

"And improve?"

"That's where you learn what you'd do differently next time."

"So if I've painted a five legged cow or missed the chimney from the farmhouse I know to fix them next time."

"Well?" Jim adds apologetically. "I did say it wouldn't fit doing a painting."

"I'm sorry I'm being flippant. I understand the process, but it feels a bit mechanical, a bit static. I'm not sure that it's going to help me create a great painting, a masterpiece."

"Well no, but this is business."

Jim wants to have said this as a joke, for it to be heard as a joke, but he knows it reflects a reality. It is a reality that smells of the disappointment that so much of the effort of business is lost in the sludge of coping. There's no time for a retraction before the artist pounces, and Jim knows that he is right.

Masterpiece

"Well maybe it's the business today, but I'm pretty sure that it wasn't the business that your great grandfather created. I'm sure that he had in mind a vision of what he wanted to create; his masterpiece. When he set off, didn't he see this as an exciting adventure, something he wanted to do, something he wanted to succeed, or why would he have done it. Why didn't he just go off and start some other business, or do something else, or just stay in bed?"

As Jim reflects on this the artist continues.

"I think I understand the process, but I'm not surprised that people didn't get excited about applying it. There's not an awful lot to get excited about, it's a bit plod, plod, plod."

He walks his fingers across the table to illustrate the plodding procession conjured up by Jim's description.

Jim can do little but agree. In fact he didn't dare confess the fact, but that's exactly how they used it. Their change meetings plodded through a four part agenda, looking at each of the steps in turn. It wasn't exciting, dealing with the challenge of change, it was an ordeal for people having to justify what they had done. As he thought, he couldn't escape the conclusion that this was another negative aspect of their picture of change-ability. The business made it an ordeal for people to propose and create change. It was much easier to sit at the back and keep quiet. Again it seemed so obvious now. He'd sat in meetings that discussed how to get more ideas from people. They'd spent hours discussing all sorts of possible options and inducements, payments, brochures and presentations. They'd agonised about the reasons for lack of suggestions, but never the simple fact that it made more sense just to keep quiet, to stay in bed as the artist had described it.

'Every vital organization owes its birth and life to an exciting and daring idea.'
James B. Conant

The artist however continued, "Thinking about it, I guess the creation of a painting follows the same sort of a process, even if you perhaps wouldn't formally write it down or describe it as such."

"I guess that I can't imagine artists going much for processes."

Jim's preconception of artists still has little space for them doing anything requiring real effort, let alone needing to plan and prepare for it.

Dream

"Maybe you'd be surprised," replied the artist "But it has to feel much more dynamic. Well where do we begin, eh planning? Ok, to start with I'd think of a painting beginning with an idea, a dream and imagination. It's about imagining what could be, creating something new, not just piecing together what you already know."

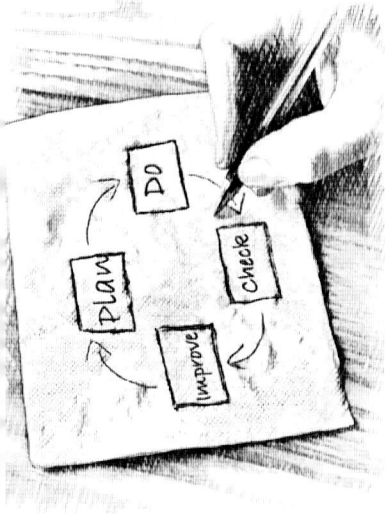

For the first time Jim notices a roughly drawn sketch of the process he has described on the folded napkin provided with the coffee. Four boxes connected in sequence in a loop, each bearing one of the words, plan, do, check and improve, sketched by the artist whilst he'd been speaking.

He watches as the artist now overwrites 'plan' with the word 'dream'.

Immediately Jim feels the connection between the word 'dream' and the new way in which he had seen the questions, posed by the artist earlier.

'When a scientist doesn't know the answer to a problem, he is ignorant. When he has a hunch as to what the result is, he is uncertain. And when he is pretty darned sure of what the result is going to be, he is in some doubt.'
Richard Feynman

His was a world dominated by answers. He'd progressed and was measured by what he knew. Questions pointed to a pigeonhole where an answer lay and was to be retrieved. Indeed so much value was attached to answers that in his world he felt compelled to provide them, even when the pigeonhole was empty. He now saw how blind he'd been to his overriding focus on answers, and how persistent the artist had to be for him to recognise that he was being questioned. Until that point, all of his answers had been the same, all pointing to what he knew, no room for anything new, no opportunity for change or even doubt. He imagined, with some

"That is what learning is. You suddenly understand something you've understood all your life, but in a new way.'
Doris Lessing

Thinking, Learning, remembering, knowing; imagining and creating new ideas; preserving and communicating knowledge over distances in time and space. Not only is it wonderful in its compass and variety; it is unique. It makes us human.'
Gilbert Highet

guilt, that when at work his defences against being questioned were even more robust, and his stock of answers dispensed even more readily.

"…. I think dreams are what we live for," the artist continued. "They're the reason to wake up in the morning with energy, fire and enthusiasm. That so many people are only allowed dreams outside work is a tragedy, as their work lives are frittered away coping rather than creating."

The idea of work filled with dreams pushes Jim a little further. Previously it would have been a push towards retreat in the comfort zone of his fixed response, the easy recognition that the artist didn't understand the realities of his world. But now this push has the opposite effect, a move towards discomfort with his old world. It felt as if the protective armour of knowing answers has been pierced, and where it has been pierced once, it may be pierced again and again. Far from the prepared repost that he would previously have used, Jim proceeds forwards just as the train, unsure of what might lay ahead. He tentatively offers,

"I know what you mean, but we need to plan, to co-ordinate things, to be able to predict what we need."

"Well maybe, but Dr Martin Luther King said I have a dream, not I have a plan."

"Yes I know, but…"

"I think he said it for good reason. I have a dream invites people to dream themselves. It's an invitation to participate, and build the dream, to feel it, not simply implement it. The dream has no boundaries, it's a balloon to be inflated with energy and will grow to be the container of this growing spirit." As the artist speaks his expression is animated and he waves his arms as if drawing the images conjured up in his minds eye.

Jim can't help but reflect how bizarre it would be to get this reaction from people invited to help with planning. It seemed to him that a qualification for involvement in planning was a total lack of imagination, a lack of energy and a lack of life. Plans so often felt to be made of dry dead tinder twigs, not green shoots of growth. 'Did people do this to planning, or did planning do this to people?' he wondered. He'd wanted to believe it was the former, to be able to blame the planners for not injecting plans with passion, but he recognised that he showed no more passion than they did when called to participate.

"The dream is a place to enjoy and to live," added the artist.

Jim was torn. He accepted the artist's words more readily that he could have imagined before they had met, but business was different. Didn't it have to have order and control?

Invitation

"The problem is that 'I have a plan' defines a framework," the artist continued, "a boundary which specifies what will be done within it, controlling and constraining your contribution. Plans do not speak to the emotions of what could be, they speak to the logic of what has been. They don't invite the creation of the future, they assemble it from pieces of the past defining what will be done, and by implication what will not.

'Life is filled with so many exciting twists and turns. Hop off the straight and narrow whenever you can and take the winding paths. Experience the exhilaration of the view from the edge. Because the moments spent there, that take your breath away, are what make you feel truly alive.'
Stacey Charter

"Yes, but surely we need sequences, schedules, instructions of what needs doing," offered Jim in defence.

"But we don't live segmented lives. We don't live in a segmented world where things can be separated, or in a stationary world that will stand still waiting for us to complete a planned task. Our world is fluid, connected and ever changing."

Jim was still struggling. Plans were the hard-won cornerstone of the business. They defined everything that was to happen. He could still remember the time before they had plans, when everything just sort of happened, or more often didn't. Did the artist really mean imagine and dream instead of planning? As tentatively as before he tested his understanding.

"I see you don't have a plan for a painting, you keep it all in your head, but for a business you have to have something written down."

"Whether it's written or not isn't important, nor is the name, it's what the name represents. You said yourself that your plans are static, dead."

"Yes, I know, but..." Static or dead, Jim thought, at least they provided the comfort of being there, of defining something, of providing some instruction.

"Do they work? Do they lead you towards a masterpiece, or just allow you to cope?" pressed the artist.

'He knows. The artist knows they let us cope. How does he know?' Jim thought to himself. 'They provide a structured way, a blame apportioning way of coping with..., with lack of success. Yes coping was avoiding failure in the main, but usually, just as assuredly avoiding success. Avoiding the masterpieces that success should be. Masterpiece?' The word rattled around his head feeling so out of place, and why? Why not think of a masterpiece? Why not contribute to a masterpiece? Yes he was right. Cope was what they did.

Without waiting for Jim to give voice to his reply the artist continued.

"Call them plans if you like, but they have to have life breathed into them, and the word 'plan' and what it represents doesn't help that. You can't expect people to get excited unless there's something exciting. Dreams stretch people, allow them to achieve, to be something."

Triggered by the word, Jim offers,

"But we have stretched targets, we want people to stretch, to achieve more."

Being

"But is that the same as wanting them to *be* more?" replied the artist. "Do these stretched targets excite people, energise them, make them feel good?"

Jim could feel the painting of another negative on the change-ability canvas, as he confessed.

"No, if truth be told they generally resent them. We try to sit down and agree them, make sure they are happy with them, explain why we've got to improve, do more, cut costs. We do all the right things, or what we've been told are right, but no they don't get excited about them. They don't seem to want to stretch."

The artist takes a moment to peel a strip of stretchy elastic glue from part of the sandwich packaging, before continuing.

"I don't think it's because they don't want to stretch and achieve, but if the targets simply add increments to last year's performance, that's not stretching towards a dream. What you are actually saying is, 'more of what you haven't bought in to, for less of what we buy you with.' This is what people refuse with stretched targets. They're about stretching the tenuous link between what they'd really like to achieve with their life, and the compromises that work forces them to make. There should be little wonder that this stretching sometimes reaches breaking point. It's not the stuff of dreams."

It's the challenge to Jim's understanding that now approaches breaking point,

"But be serious. I can't tell people to stop planning and start dreaming."

The artist waited a moment before saying,

"What was your grandfather doing ninety-eight years ago. Wasn't he following a dream?"

Jim felt his armour pierced again, but his defences tried to fight back. He knew that at the start the business wasn't run by plans. But that was ninety-eight years ago, things have changed, and they've grown. What worked for a small business couldn't work for a bigger one. He felt it; the piercing of his armour. Were these just more well rehearsed responses, extractions from the pigeon holes of what he thought he already knew. Maybe on the painting of his grandfather there was something, something that enabled the business to succeed and grow, something that they couldn't see, but thought they could paint as something to do, plans and a planning process. Their planning was an attempt to create something that his great grandfather was, but had they painted it badly. Had the way they planned for the future, itself begun to destroy the ability they once had for moving successfully into that future?

He remembered the arguments, ten years previously, to introduce structured plans. He'd led them. Things were chaotic, they needed to be controlled, he'd championed planning - and now the thought that he might be championing their removal or their transformation. As the artist had said, it's not the word, but what it represents, and the word 'plan' represented all that was dry and dead in a static world that had no real understanding of change.

'The purpose of Art is to create enthusiasm.'
Picasso

118

It wasn't that writing things down was bad, or that agreeing what to do was bad. It was that they thought that doing plans was of itself good. That was what was wrong. They'd never had sight of what they needed to move forward successfully, they'd never seen the picture of the company's change-ability, so they'd guessed.

He thought about their planning process painted on the change-ability canvas. However much he tried, it proved impossible to imagine it painted other than as a disability.

He felt a flood of uncertainty sweep across him, a chill down his spine; what his grandmother had told him when he was young was 'someone walking over his grave'. The words of course weren't to be taken literally, but today those words connected with the deadness of plans and the future, the place you're going to. Someone walking over the grave of the business.

The chill he felt reflected his uncertainty. The things he held to be true, his world held to be true, were falling away as the ice melted, and in their place nothing solid. In place of the comforting reassurance of the solid ice floes beneath his feet, was water. Not a different place, but a different way of being.

The fear of what this canvas, if painted, would reveal was now very real. Saturday morning pouring over the contents of his briefcase would provide no defence. Working late, working hard provided no safety. He needed to understand this new picture of the business.

Stretch

The artist had continued speaking, oblivious to the questions spinning in Jim's mind. Jim wasn't sure that he needed to hear any more. His, and the company's understanding of even this simplest of processes beyond what they did, was already clearly demolished. He looked for something to happen, something to distract the conversation. The train continued to creep forwards. He willed it to accelerate, or to stop, anything that demanded they pay attention to it. His hands were raised in surrender, but the artist had moved on to the next step in the process Jim had introduced.

'The past is of no importance. The present is of no importance. It is with the future that we have to deal. For the past is what man should not have been. The present is what man ought not to be. The future is what artists are.'
Oscar Wilde

"I wouldn't think of 'do' when creating a painting. I'd think of 'stretching', trying to reach some new point, some new level. If the process is about change, creating something new, then you don't simply do what you planned, but go beyond it. The idea of stretching conveys the 'not knowing in advance'. Change is about taking steps into the unknown. If you step into the known it's not change. It may be new to you, but that's a measure of your ignorance not of your imagination. Your dreams will not be served if they are constrained to actions that are chosen from a menu of the past. When you stretch, you can't know the outcome."

"Not know the outcome?" replied Jim, desperation reflected in his voice.

It was the same message, drawing him, pulling him away from the comforting certainty of knowledge, of well rehearsed answers and the security of data, and towards this place of not knowing.

'When the artist is alive in any person, whatever his kind of work may be, he becomes an inventive, searching, daring, self-expressing, creature. He becomes interesting to other people. He disturbs, upsets, enlightens and he opens the way for a better understanding.'
Robert Henri

"That's what the future feels like." continued the artist. "The future is the unknown. When it's known it's simply a piece of the past that has yet to happen, it's not the future. The word stretch means excitement, discovery, challenge."

Jim plays with the expression 'a piece of the past that has yet to happen', toying with what this might mean.

The artist strikes through the word 'do' on the napkin and replaces it with 'stretch', as he continues.

"You stretch with your senses honed for action, ears pricked, eyes keen, muscles tensed ready for excitement. This is the dynamic. Stretching isn't the mechanical trotting out of a planned schedule, plodding along a known course. It's testing yourself; maybe you will succeed, maybe you won't. It's being alive ready to experience, ready to learn, not the stale reliving of something already done, the cloning of previous experience, yours or another's."

The artist senses a note of alarm in Jim's expression and attempts to allay what he's sees as the cause.

"It feels risky, but don't mistake this for foolhardy. It's a world of keen and alert, responsive and awake, part of a living cycle, not a mechanistic step as part of a ritual."

Once more Jim is triggered by a key word.

"But we manage risk. We have risk planning meetings."

As the words leave his lips, the pieces of understanding fall into place. He wishes he can recall the words before they are heard, but too late he realises the strength of his reflex of taking answers and launching them from their pigeon holes.

The artist is now in full stride as he continues,

"You may think your life has no place for risk; lives at stake, dangers to avoid, and mouths to feed. In a changing world, we might risk

'We pay a heavy price for our fear of failure. It is a powerful obstacle to growth. It assures the progressive narrowing of the personality and prevents exploration and experimentation. There is no learning without some difficulty and fumbling. If you want to keep on learning, you must keep on risking failure -- all your life.'
John W. Gardner

much more by plodding the proven steps of the past, than with new steps based on what is, not what was. It is easy for our blinkers to fall across our eyes as we excuse ourselves from the vibrancy of life, by obligations and commitments. Stretching doesn't mean reckless, but it equally doesn't mean what we have always known to be safe. Too often we wait until the tried and tested fails, before trying and learning the new."

For Jim this described their business. Leaving things as they are, hoping things will continue to work and springing into action to fix things when they break. There was no reaching, no stretching, just doing, doing, fixing and doing. 'He's right.' Thought Jim, 'do is the plod to follow plan, the mechanical grinding out of a backward looking plan. Stretch feels like the reaching forward into the excitement of our dreams.'

'It is not death that a man should fear, but he should fear never beginning to live.' Marcus Aurelius

Sense

"Ok now this is where I look out for five legged cows." The artist says with a wink as he adds a mutant cow to the napkin sketch. Alongside he crosses out the word 'check' to be replaced by 'sense'.

"Rather than check that you've done things correctly, I think you have to be much more alive. You're not following a recipe, instead you are trying to sense what's really happening, what is it that you are creating."

"I guess if there is no plan."

"Well I didn't say there'd be no plan." corrects the artist

"OK, a plan that's not fixed, a dynamic plan, a dream, then there's not a fixed checklist to check against."

"That's right. This is not about checking that what happened is what you expected. Nor even is it just checking in the areas where you expected there to be effects. This is an acknowledgement that you have tried something and can't know what its effects will be. You are not looking in specific areas for results. You are opening yourself up to sense and appreciate the consequences of what you have created."

"Consequences?" queried Jim, smiling as he finds the word strangely attractive.

"Yes, I kind of like thinking of them as consequences. Again it's the idea of not knowing, the fact that you may have achieved any manner of things, some of them quite unexpected. That feels much more like someone going to work to create a masterpiece."

"I guess so. So it's not checking, it's sensing."

'What is important is to keep learning, to enjoy challenge, and to tolerate ambiguity. In the end there are no certain answers.'
Martina Horner.

"I think so, because sense conveys that the nature of the effect you have may take any form. It may be sensed by sight, touch, or any other means and whilst it may take tangible form as something you can easily measure, it may also appear less tangible as an impression felt, or something indirect, only seen through its impact elsewhere. Sense is the invitation to maximise the learning from the experiment of stretching to try to create a dream."

"Sensing to find out what you can learn?" Jim couldn't help but warm to the idea. It all made sense, disturbing tough the contrast was with his previous perception of his 'real world'.

"It's why I listen to music," explained the artist as he points to the earpieces of the I-pod still draped on his chest. "You'd be surprised, but the solution to many a problem may be sitting inside a piece of music."

The artist reflects for a moment, as if recalling a particular tune, before continuing.

"It is the opposite of a sterile anticipation of the result you knew, or hoped that you would create. Sensing is being alive to the double blind test for life."

The artist adds as if to reveal the essence to himself,

"Accepting that you don't know what you don't know."

Jim feels the urge to interrupt as a piece of understanding falls into place.

Questions

"That's why you don't like portraits and landscapes!"

"Eh?"

"Well because they don't stretch the viewer to think. You either recognise them or don't, and categorise them as good or bad before moving on."

'It's not what you look at that matters, it's what you see.'
Henry David Thoreau

"I didn't say I didn't like them…"

"No but you don't like them to be seen as answers, you like to see questions."

"That's true. It's the way that you see them that's important. Learning has to be dynamic, the act of questioning, the verb, not the collection of answers as nouns."

It dawns on Jim. "So that was it! You didn't like the way I looked at portraits and landscapes?" asked Jim.

The artist has no need to answer, his point is made.

Jim thinks for a moment about seeing a portrait, not as an answer to the question of who it represents, but as a question asking who they are. Same portrait. The change is in the person viewing.

"I see that." Jim says, giving voice to the thought. "I think I see it. It seems like quite a small difference, but it's actually huge."

"In some ways yes. A small change on the outside can be the sign of a big change inside a person." agrees the artist.

Jim begins to appreciate how large this difference in the understanding of questions can be.

His thinking drifts again to life inside his business,

"We have lots of questions in business, but we only really value answers."

He ponders the thought for a moment before adding,

"Our questions are really just labels for answers. We think we understand questions, but we're not seeing them as dynamic, as about the future. They're labels for what we know, not tools to explore what we don't."

He thinks how big and how small this change in their thinking might be, and the opportunities it might create.

Grow

Without them realising it, the train has gradually picked up speed, and for the first time the artist is conscious his stop may soon be approaching. He is keen to complete his description, and hastily replaces the word 'improve' with 'grow', and resumes his description.

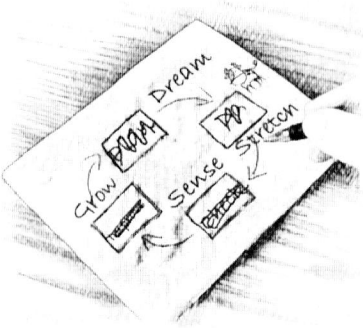

"Rather than just improving what you've found, which may amount to little more than changing what you do, grow means becoming something you weren't, through the experience of what you've done."

"So what you are, not what you do." Jim replies acknowledging the shift from doing to being.

"Yes, grow is the culmination of learning. Change is not about what we have done, it is about what we have become. We are not an accumulation of everything we have done, rather we are the consequence of the effects of everything we have experienced."

"So change is about learning, and learning is about what we are, and not what we do." Jim seeks confirmation of his new understanding.

"I think so. We should measure what we did, not by looking at the doing, but the being. What did we become by it? What's important is what we are, what we're being."

Jim shakes his head as he replies, "But this isn't the way we normally think."

"You're right. For most of us we think of doing, and it feels a little strange to think of being. When someone returns from a holiday we ask 'what did you do?' This is kind of the wrong question. What did I do? I went to the beach, I saw a church, I rode in a boat. We need to ask how you are different. How have you grown from the experience. What are you capable of that you were not. This is the measure of change."

"Yes, but it sounds weird," confessed Jim with a smile. "What did you become on holiday?"

"For a holiday perhaps. But if we're thinking about change, if you haven't changed then your visit to the beach is irrelevant, it didn't happen. The real question is not whether you left footprints on the beach, but did the beach leave footprints on you?"

Again Jim feels the knife's incisive cut between being and doing. "Change within me."

"Exactly," confirms the artist. "The word growth perfectly captures this. Don't be afraid to use it and don't replace it with irrelevant descriptions of actions. Change isn't the coat that you wear, a gesture you can make, an action that you can buy. Change is growth whether positive or negative."

"But don't I grow by doing things?" Jim still senses the voice within him still struggling to see being, except through what he does.

"Of course you might do things, but it's not the doing that is important. Take for example attending a training course."

"Doing!" Jim interjects.

"Ok a training course you do. It shouldn't be measured by what you did, but by what you became."

Jim's less than convinced expression prompts the artist to provide another example.

Changing

"This conversation is not measured by how much you listened or heard or said, but by how much you were changed. If you weren't changed by it, then you might just as well have not done it. In fact you didn't do it. If you weren't changed, you didn't do the training course and you didn't have this conversation."

'I shut my eyes and all the world drops dead; I lift my eyes and all is born again.'
Sylvia Plath

'Didn't do it?' Jim ponders this thought for a moment thinking of training courses he's done without gaining anything, yes perhaps without doing them. It seems that many fall into this category. He spent the time, or the time was spent, but ok maybe he didn't really do them.

The thought suddenly crystallises in Jim's mind.

"It's the thing with the tree in the forest isn't it?"

"You what?" asks the artist somewhat surprised.

"The thing, you must know; if a tree falls in the forest and no one is there to hear it, did it really fall?"

"Erm, I guess, maybe?"

"I see what you mean though, even if I sat through it, read through all the notes, listened to all the words, if I didn't learn anything, then I didn't do it."

He imagines another negative on the company's changeability painting, this time their system for evaluating training which captures attendance, quality of handouts, impressions, but nothing of being changed. He feels no need to interrupt the artist to share this, as he's now convinced that he appreciates how bleak a picture of change-ability he would paint.

'You must constantly ask yourself these questions: Who am I around? What are they doing to me? What have they got me reading? What have they got me saying? Where do they have me going? What do they have me thinking? And most important, what do they have me becoming? Then ask yourself the big question: Is that okay? Your life does not get better by chance, it gets better by change.'
Jim Rohn

"Grow is again all about the unknown. You can't know the future until you experience it when it becomes the present, and you make sense of what you experience. This can be the perpetuation of yesterday, or the doorway to tomorrow."

Jim desperately wants some time to think through what he's just learned. He picks up the coffee cup and glares at its unappetising contents, which seem only to glare back at him, defying him to drink them. He buys a few moments by bringing the cup to his lips and tipping it, though not quite far enough to allow its uninviting contents to make contact with his lips. He holds it there for a moment or two before conceding defeat.

His thoughts swirl. He likes the dynamic, is energised by the thought, and the artist's description has breathed life into the long dead carcass of his chairman's idea of PDCI. But business is different. Business is the real world. Business doesn't feel like this, can't feel like this.

"I can see that process applied to a painting, and I can see that it's more energetic and alive, but for business? I just don't think it would work." He reads from the napkin, "Dream Stretch, Sense, Grow, it just doesn't feel right."

The artist pauses for a moment before responding.

"The point is, it's exactly the same process. It is Plan, Do, Check, Improve. It's the identical process. It's not that the words are different, the words are irrelevant."

"But you've written the words in. Aren't the words important?"

'You can become blind by seeing each day as a similar one. Each day is a different one, each day brings a miracle of its own. It's just a matter of paying attention to this miracle.'
Paulo Coelho

"If I could, I wouldn't even use words to describe it. As soon as you use words, people focus on them. They switch off thinking about what it means, and just start doing the words. They stop being, stop thinking, and slink back into doing. Doing planning, or doing dreaming, it won't make any difference, it's the doing that's wrong.

My words might shock people for a moment, perhaps as they shock you, but they'd soon shape the words to tell them what to do. What is different are the eyes through which it is seen, and the way in which it is felt. No words can bring it to life for eyes that can only see plod, plod, plod, and no words can kill if for eyes that are alive. It's the same process. What determines its nature are the eyes through which it is seen. That's absolutely all that's different."

Jim thinks of 'the eyes through which it's seen.' He wants to embrace the artist's description, but something holds him back, painfully restraining him from accepting.

Sensing this, the artist turns the knife,

"Are you saying that business isn't alive?"

Jim feels the pain of recognition not only that it isn't alive, but that he hasn't even been aware of the lack of life. Indeed the pain grows deeper as he recognises previously being unaware even of the question. He's been sucked into a world of doing, which killed questioning so effectively, that he never even saw it die.

He'd said that they'd gone through the motions with plan, do, check and improve. They squeezed the life from it, killed the spirit and buried it so deeply, that no one could suspect that it had once had a vibrant beating heart. It is the roaring tiger, shot, stuffed and its head mounted on a wall. If you point and ask, people answer 'tiger', but it bears little relation to the animal that once lived.

But it was much worse even than this. They went through the motions with so much more of what they did. This was but a symptom of the lack of life throughout everything they did as they plod, plod plodded through their days.

He's suddenly immersed in a sense of guilt. His work, the major focus of his life, in many ways defining his real world. His family have been important, of course they have, and he loves them dearly. But in a sense they sit outside his real world, an intrusion, a welcome and loved intrusion, but an intrusion none the less. His family are the evidence of another world, but not what he's felt as his real world, the world that gives him meaning.

'God is really only another artist. He invented the giraffe, the elephant and the cat. He has no real style, He just goes on trying other things.'
Pablo Picasso

But now his real world is shaken and threatened; undermined by something as simple as a painting. In truth it's taken, not even that, simply questions about a painting to rock its foundations. His real world has been exposed as a nether world where you just don't feel emotions, don't feel alive. A place where you do things, do what you're told and tell others to do.

He thinks of how he described PDCI before the artist so comprehensively redefined it. 'The do step is the main part of the process.' This seems to capture his world of work, no time for dreaming, stretching or growing, just doing. And with this he feels deep within him that this doing, however well and however much, provides nothing at all to assure the future.

Does it have to be like that? Does it have to be so lifeless? These were questions he wanted to ask. But even now a voice inside him was saying we need plans, control, direction. We need to manage, budget, define and programme. So instead he found himself saying,

"We could lighten up a bit I'll grant you, but business isn't art. We need plans, we need controls, someone has to direct what's going to happen, how else are we to achieve anything."

As he spoke he felt the falseness of his words and the frailty of his plans. He waited for the artist to remind him of his admission that his plans were dead. He felt the incompatibility of his plea for control and the lack of control he really felt; the fear that the business may be swept aside at anytime; the feeling that he could do nothing to prevent it happening or even to see it coming. He knew all of this, yet still the voice said 'business is different'. He waited for the artist to demolish his argument, to throw it back at him.

Nature   But the artist simply said, "This is what nature does."

Jim, who'd prepared to defend his corner as best he could, was left bemused.

"Nature?"

"You said, how could you be expected to achieve anything?

"Yes. Without plans to direct everyone, how will anything get done? How will things come together, be coordinated for example?"

"Well think of nature or evolution. Evolution doesn't have a plan. It tries things, new things, different things, sometimes crazy things, earthquakes, mutations, volcanoes, fires. They're things that we might find ourselves calling disasters or mistakes. And then it sees what happens. It lives. It lets them run their course. Then it learns, sometimes they work, and sometimes they don't. If they work it keeps them, remembers them and builds on them. If they don't then it gets rid of them sooner or later."

"But evolution? I mean. Well it's just not …" The thought of comparing business to evolution sends Jim's mind spinning as he struggles to identify an appropriate pigeon hole for an answer.

"Evolution has created everything you see, everything you sense, everything you are," continues the artist. "And all it had for raw material was a cloud of gas. That's all there was, in the first moments of the universe.

In eleven billion years, evolution it's turned the sparsest imaginable raw materials into all of this, into all of you. Just by a willingness to stretch, to sense, learn and to grow."

"Yes but you don't understand business, the pace of change, the difficulties…"

"Evolution began with almost nothing. There simply was nothing else. Imagine that. There was nothing else, no stars, no planets, no earth, no universe, no life, just nothing, absolutely nothing. It's difficult for us even to imagine the nothingness without imagining a something to hold it.. And from that nothingness it created everything."

'Yes but business is different.' The thought now lacking the energy of conviction is left unspoken as the artist continues.

"Your start point is a company filled with the most intelligent beings in the known universe. The culmination of that eleven billion years of evolution is at your disposal. All the things it has created. True you don't have eleven billion years but if you look at what a cloud of gas has achieved, what do you think you might achieve with the same process?"

The voice of old thinking in his head still wanted Jim to resist, to press the case for the difference. Though on the scale of change the artist had laid before him there could be no difference, the voice still demanded he represent it.

"Ok I see evolution stretches, senses and grows, but where does evolution dream?"

Dreams

This felt like the voice's last ditched attempt to unpick the argument.

"Just look around you at the unimaginable variety, beauty and complexity of the world. Don't you think that is the product of dreams?

'Nobody succeeds beyond his or her wildest expectations unless he or she begins with some wild expectations.'
Ralph Charell

You see if you do the other steps you, can't help but engage your imagination. You can't truly stretch without imagining where you may reach. You can't sense without truly imagining what you may encounter, or grow without imagining what your experiences have revealed. Evolution, nature, is all a process of dreaming."

Jim takes a minute to reflect. He's been drawn into wildly unfamiliar territory. What began as a gentle conversation to while away time, became a project, a solution, the answer to a problem. But then he'd glimpsed that his real need was not for a new answer, but a new way of seeing. But this new way of seeing was itself unfamiliar territory. It was seeing by not seeing, seeing not through answers that describe, but through questions that open up. Value placed not on knowing, but on not knowing. And now he understood the nature of this new territory. It was a place for thinking, and it was indeed unfamiliar.

Jim fell silent whilst he reflected on what he'd become. Eventually he asked the question,

"This isn't just how you paint a picture is it, this process?"

"No. It's the way I see, the way I approach everything."

"The artist's way?"

"If that's what you like to call it."

"Even work? It's the way you'd approach work, and not just painting."

"Why not? Fantasy, imagination, dreaming are words that we have excluded from our business vocabularies. They have been consigned to the world of play and of art, as if they have no part in the serious world of our business or working lives. We can't have fun, without feeling guilty that it isn't real work."

He holds up the earpiece to his I-pod.

"We can't listen to music without it being the company song! That so many people achieve so much in their hobbies and pastimes, yet feel they can contribute so little to their time spent at work, should ring a huge alarm bell. Business isn't a special case, somewhere elevated above the realms of human emotion. Being alive is what's special, and for most of us the only thing special about work, is that we're not expected to be alive."

The artist stares out of the carriage window and into the now black star lit sky.

"Imagination and dreaming are not just the kindling for the fire from which new ideas originate, they are the source of energy with which to turn these new ideas into future realities. Most of us achieve so little in our working lives, because that is precisely what we and our businesses set out to achieve. We need to dream."

He looks Jim in the eye as he adds. "Don't use the word coyly, this is not the sterile process of planning, this is the joyous shouting from the rooftops that magic is going to take place, and the invitation to people to come and make it happen."

Jim's head is spinning with new imagery the artist's words have conjured.

"It would be good if work were like that." He agrees and questions at one and the same time.

'Life is not a journey to the grave with the intention of arriving safely in a pretty and well preserved body...... but rather to skid in broadside, thoroughly used up, totally worn out, and loudly proclaiming... 'Wow! That was one hell of a ride"
Anon.

"We have the opportunity to do great things with our lives, to create new worlds." the artist replied. "With our eyes open there is no limit to what we can achieve, yet with our eyes closed we fritter away our time, squeezing the life out of our existence."

Jim seems lost in thought for a moment before responding, "I hear what you say, but I just can't imagine doing great things. I mean life's just too difficult just getting by."

The artist looks Jim in the eye.

"It's wrong to think that great things are done by great people. That's just the way we choose to see them once something great has happened. We look at what was done, and confuse that with who they are. It's this same confusion of being and doing."

Jim's puzzled expression signals the artist to continue.

"You can be great. You aren't what you do, and you aren't what you can't do, or think you can't do. You can do anything."

"Oh yeh?"

"Of course. Absolutely you are." The artist pauses for a moment before adding "Just imagine someone great, a writer, Shakespeare.

Even he wasn't born with a pen in his hand. He wasn't a writer, but imagine one day he picked up a pen and wrote something. The next day he still wasn't a writer, but he wrote something else, and the next and the next. He still wasn't a writer, but he was writing.

So you might ask, when did he become a writer?

Well maybe he was writing for a thousand days and he still wasn't a writer. Then perhaps he thought to himself. I spend a lot of time writing, I'm a writer."

"You mean he just decided?" responded Jim dismissively.

"Well why not? Then he perhaps thought to himself I didn't become a writer today. I'm the same as I was yesterday. I was a writer yesterday too. In fact I was a writer all of those thousand days. I was a writer from the day I picked up a pen. But I wasn't different on that day either. All I did was pick up a pen. I've been a writer all of my life, and if I never write another word, I'll be a writer till the day I die."

Jim thinks for a moment, trying to tease out the flaw in the artist's argument. Disappointed that he fails to do so, he responds lamely with, "Yes but he was a writer."

"Yes, but as I said, he was a writer before he picked up a pen," replied the artist.

"I know, he was a natural, had a talent for it."

"No you miss the point. He was a writer before he picked up a pen, and would have been if he'd never picked up a pen."

"How?"

"Because he was who he was, and decided he was a writer."

"Yes but I'm not Shakespeare!"

"The point is that neither was he. If he'd never picked up a pen, he wouldn't have written a word, but he was still a writer. He decided that he was a writer, not the publishers, not the critics, or readers. He decided. Maybe he also decided that he was a painter. Perhaps he never picked up a paintbrush, but he was a painter, and an architect, and a sailor."

"I'm not ..."

"I just think that to write the way he did, he had a way of seeing things that wasn't driven by him limiting what he could be. He was driven by believing that he could be, and was everything. He didn't spend his days telling himself what he couldn't be. Maybe if he'd turned a different corner, had a different thought, heard a different piece of music that day, he'd have picked up a paintbrush and spoken to the world through pigment, rather than through words.

"So he was a really talented guy?"

"No. We are all really talented people. All of us. Every moment we tell ourselves, think to ourselves that we can't, we chip away at that talent, erode its power and lower our sights so that pretty soon we're just happy to cope."

He looks Jim in the eye before adding,

"We all have the ability."

"Our change-ability." offers Jim.

"Yes, that's the secret. It's the secret your great grandfather had, and that you must have. He could paint the picture for the company, and so must you."

"But painting it?" Though he sees the value of this painting, the means to create it seem just as far out of reach.

'To the question of your life you are the answer, and to the problems of your life you are the solution.'
Joe Cordare

A high pitched whine signalled the application of the brakes, and with this the carriage vibrated and set the remaining coffee dancing in rings within the cups.

The artist stands and scans out into the blackness and sees the telltale pattern of dots of light, like fallen stars scattered against the landscape, that signal the approach to his stop.

The carriage is suddenly transformed into a sea of movement as people, long constrained to inactivity, reach for belongings and put on coats in preparation for the cool night air. The comforting illusion of the permanence of their world within the carriage is dispelled in an instant.

"But the painting?" asks Jim.

All thought of the centenary had been forgotten. Jim was now desperate to know how you could paint this picture of change-ability.

"The painting. Can you paint our change-ability?" Jim pleads.

'A man paints with his brains and not with his hands.'
Michelangelo

"I couldn't do that," replies the artist, stepping back to allow the rugby supporter to squeeze past him.

Jim is enveloped in a sense of anger and disappointment.

"But why not?"

"There's no need," he replies as he pulls a small bag from the luggage rack above his head. As he does a small piece of paper flutters towards the floor unseen.

The train lurches to a halt and the artist offers his hand towards Jim,

"It's been a pleasure to meet you and learn about your business."

The handshake is over. He turns towards the door and is carried along the aisle amidst the trail of departing passengers.

Jim's mind is racing, "No need, there's no need?" he shouts.

Amid the bobbing heads the artist turns and replies, "You've already begun to see differently. You're painting it yourself."

As he turns his head to go, he adds, "Keep painting."

See differently

As Jim tries to understand, the artist is out through the door. He scans the pools of light on the platform, looking, needing one last clue, one more word, but there is no sign of the artist. With a lurch the train is back in motion. Cupped hand against the glass he peers out towards the platform, turning and straining forlornly for one last glimpse amongst the image of his reflection, before turning back towards the stillness of the carriage.

'The moment you think you understand a great work of art, it's dead for you.'
Robert Wilson

On the Formica table he sees the folded napkin, four boxes with crossed out contents, the five legged cow and the words Dream, Stretch, Sense and Grow. And beneath the picture is written something else. He spins the napkin around to face him and reads, 'Paint it with questions'. And beneath it 'Being not Doing'.

The train is now picking up speed, its uncertainty left behind as it heads into the darkness. He is suddenly aware of his surroundings. The carriage is almost empty and now all he hears is the rhythmic rattle of the wheels as they mark the progress along the track.

Soon it is his turn to see a familiar pattern of lights, like the stars that guide mariners, signalling that home draws near. He picks up the napkin, 'Paint it with questions.'

'The job is to ask questions - it always was - and to ask them as inexorably as I can. And to face the absence of precise answers with a certain humility.'
Arthur Miller

As the train begins to brake he reaches up to retrieve his coat and notices a piece of paper lodged in the cushion of the artist's seat. He retrieves it, 'Bryan Foster, Managing Director, Foster Electronic Systems. Designers and Manufacturers of Electronic Control Equipment.'

He reads it again. ' .... Electronic Control Equipment?' before popping the card into his shirt pocket.

'Paint it with questions.' he thinks.

He can't help but laugh out loud. 'Of course it's not a painting,' he thinks, and mocking himself chuckles as he repeats, 'painting, paints, easel, artist, the works! It's a way of seeing. And why shouldn't I paint it?'

There's a feint squeal of brakes as the train comes to a halt. As he opens the carriage door the cool night air envelops him.

'Do not quit. You see, the most constant state of an artist is uncertainty. You must face confusion, self-questioning, dilemma. Only amateurs are confident ... be prepared to live with the fear of failure all your art life.'
W. O. Mitchell

It's almost midnight when he reaches home. Sarah, his wife greets him at the door and receives a special hug.

"It's good to see you. Problems with the train again? What sort of a week have you had?"

"Do you know, I'm not quite sure. Maybe I'll find out, but never mind that. Tell me what you've been up to, and the kids, what have they been doing?"

'Paint it with questions' he thinks.

"I'm just making some coffee if you want one. You must be tired if you don't want to tell me how bad things have been. It isn't something serious is it?"

"What?"

"You've not been fired or something?" she asks not looking up from the task of stirring the coffee.

'When I say artist I mean the man who is building things -- creating moulding the earth -- whether it be the plains of the west -- or the iron ore of Penn. It's all a big game of construction -- some with a brush -- some with a shovel – some choose a pen.'
Jackson Pollock

'Living is a form of not being sure, not knowing what next or how. The moment you know how, you begin to die a little. The artist never entirely knows. We guess. We may be wrong, but we take leap after leap in the dark.'
Agnes de Mille

"No. Don't be silly. It can wait. I'm just interested in what you've all been up to."

"Robert's made the school football team and Jenny's done this for you."

She points to a painting attached to the front of the fridge by a magnet. "It's a picture of …"

"A picture, that's great."

"What do you mean?"

"Nothing. That's really great. Brilliant."

"Ok" she says slightly bemused, "It's a picture of …"

But before she can describe it, he interrupts. "No. I'd like her to tell me all about it tomorrow."

"Ok. I'll tell her as soon as you get your work out of the way in the morning."

"Actually I think I'll skip the work tomorrow morning."

Sarah spins around to confront him "You haven't! You haven't been fired. Is that it?"

"Is that what you think, just because I'm going to leave my papers in their briefcase?"

"Well the last time you", and then realising just when the last time was, she cries out "You haven't got a new job have you! Oh darling, I'm sorry, is that it and I thought you'd …"

"No, no, I've told you. Don't be silly. I've not got a new job and I've not been fired. I just need a bit of time for thinking. I need to do some imagining and thinking of questions, and I think Jenny can teach me a thing or two."

"Well I don't know what it means, but if you want questions, you're going to the expert. Here's your coffee."

Sarah takes a sip from hers and adds, "Well if you haven't been fired, or promoted, then something's happened or you've been working too hard!"

'Creativity is essentially a lonely art. An even lonelier struggle. To some a blessing. To others a curse. It is in reality the ability to reach inside yourself and drag forth from your very soul an idea.'
Lou Dorfsman

"Yes. And what I need is a big hug."

As they hug he feels the business card through the fabric of the shirt pocket, and taking it out, reads on the reverse in handwriting.

'Dream small, fail small. Dream big, achieve big.'

"What's that?" Sarah asks.

"Oh, just something to think about."

'Paint it with questions. Not of what you do, but of what you are. Not what you're doing, but being. Yes, what you're being', he thinks.

'We never stop investigating. We are never satisfied that we know enough to get by. Every question we answer leads on to another question. This has become the greatest survival trick of our species.'

Desmond Morris

Becoming

When we really embrace change, we become
change.

This is the most wonderful and challenging
place to be.

Wonderful, because each day we have the
opportunity to emerge from the chrysalis of our
past.

Each day we can spread new wings, take new
flight and visit new lands.

Challenging because as the butterfly emerging
from the chrysalis, all of our experience is of
being a caterpillar.

Fellow Travellers

*"For those who
know how to read,
I have painted my
autobiography."*
Pablo Picasso

The quotations are the outstretched hand of fellow travellers on the journey of change. They are drawn from people from a wide range of backgrounds.

The same thoughts can be found echoed in the words of a scientist, painted in the colours of an artist, or sung to the tune of a composer.

Contributors

17	Frank Moore Colby	American educator, writer and Professor of Economics, 1865 – 1925.
19	Henri Matisse	French painter, draftsman, printmaker and sculptor, 1869 – 1954.
24	Norio Ohga	President of Sony Electronics, originally trained as an Opera Singer, born 1930.
25	Pablo Picasso	Spanish painter and sculptor, 1881 – 1973.
25	Confucius	Chinese thinker and social philosopher, 551 – 479 B.C.
27	Claude Lévi-Strauss	French anthropologist who developed structuralism as a way of understanding human society and culture, born 1908.
30	Jiddu. Krishnamurti	Indian writer and speaker on philosophical and spiritual subjects. Winner of the UN Peace Medal, 1895 – 1986.
32	Thomas Pynchon	American writer, known for his dense and complex works of fiction, born 1937.
41	Naguib Mahfouz	Egyptian novelist and winner of the Nobel Prize for Literature, 1911 – 2006.
43	John Anthony Ciardi	Poet, translator and etymologist, 1816 – 1986.
44	Hebrew Proverb	
46	Martin Luther King Jr	Civil rights leader, 1929 – 1968.

47	Voltaire	François-Marie Arouet. French enlightenment writer, essayist, deist and philosopher, 1694 – 1778.
51	Miguel de Unamuno	Spanish essayist, novelist, poet, playwright and philosopher, 1864 – 1936.
58	Nikos Kazantzakis	Greek writer of poems, novels, essays, plays and travel books. Author of 'Zorba the Greek', 1883 – 1957
59	Paul Valery	French poet, essayist and philosopher, 1871 - 1945
65	Antoine de Saint Exupéry	French writer and aviator. Author of 'The Little Prince', 1900 - 1944
67	James Arthur Baldwin	American novelist, short story writer, playwright, essayist and poet, 1924 - 1987
69 & 73	Leonard Bernstein	American conductor, composer and pianist, 1918 - 1990
77	Denis Waitley	Writer, speaker and productivity consultant.
78	Frank Dick	British former sports coach and motivational speaker,
79	George Land	Author, speaker, consultant and general systems scientist.
80	Michael Dell	Founder and CEO of Dell Computers, born 1965
82	Oliver Wendell Holmes	Member of the US Supreme Court, 1841 - 1935
82	Anne Rice	American author of gothic and religious fiction, born 1941

Contributors

121	Robert Henri	American painter, 1865 – 1929.
122	John W. Gardner	US Secretary of Health, Education and Welfare, 1912 – 2002.
123	Marcus Aurelius	Roman emperor. Last of the 'Five Good Emperors', and stoic philosopher, 121 – 180.
124	Martina Horner	President of Radcliffe College.
126	Henry David Thoreau	American author, naturalist transcendentalist, tax resister, development critic and philosopher, 1817 – 1862.
130	Sylvia Plath	Poet, novelist and short story writer, 1932 – 1963.
132	Jim Rohn	Motivational speaker and author
133	Paulo Coelho	Brazilian lyricist and novelist, born 1947.
135	Pablo Picasso	Spanish painter and sculptor, 1881 – 1973.
139	Ralph Charell	Writer
140	Tom Francesconi	Artist and teacher
140	Robert Frost	American poet and quadruple Pulitzer Prize winner, 1874 – 1963.
145	Joe Cordare	
146	Michelangelo	Italian renaissance painter, sculptor, architect, poet and engineer, 1475 – 1564.
147	Robert Wilson	Avant-garde stage director and playwright, born 1941.
148	Arthur Miller	Pulitzer Prize winning playwright and essayist, 1915 – 2005.

149	W. O. Mitchell	Canadian writer, 1914 – 1998.
150	Jackson Pollock	Influential painter in the abstract impressionist movement, 1912 – 1956.
150	Agnes de Mile	American dancer and choreographer, 1905 – 1993.
151	Lou Dorfsman	Vice President and Director of Creative Design at CBS.
152	Desmond Morris	British zoologist and ethologist, born 1928.
155	Pablo Picasso	Spanish painter and sculptor, 1881 – 1973.

About the Author

Steve Unwin has a background as a chartered engineer. Having spent ten years developing software for the aerospace industry he turned his systems thinking towards the question of organisational change.

In 1999 he received the prestigious UK Excellence Award in recognition of this work. Since 2001 he has focused on the development and sharing of insightful ideas on change, and is a regular speaker at conferences worldwide.

The following pages show some of Steve's other books available from photonbooks.com.

Steve lives in Preston England with his family of three children.

www.steveunwin.com

Letting go.

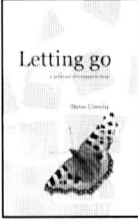

ISBN 978-1-906420-00-0

Real change happens not through what we do, but who we become. Change who we are, and there is no turning back and nothing can remain the same.

In Letting go we explore the universal truths and challenges, and share the fears and the exhilaration that real change can bring. Illuminated with over 80 carefully selected quotations.

Essence of Da Vinci

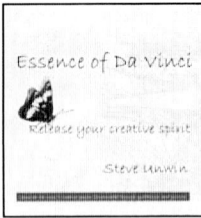

ISBN 978-1-906420-02-4

Inspired by Leonardo Da Vinci's thinking style, this insightful and wide ranging collection of quotations, taken from more modern times, illustrates the impact of creative genius in all walks of life. Supported by specially created drawings, the quotations serve to inspire the creative soul that lurks within all of us.

Featuring over 100 drawings and 250 quotations this is a treasury of insightful prompts to a more creative life.

Himalayan Odyssey

ISBN 978-1-906420-03-1

A collection of thought provoking quotations and sketches inspired by a gathering of special people in the Himalayan mountains of Nepal.

With delegates from 15 countries, 'Asian Camp' shared and explored the latest ideas on creating successful change. Himalayan Odyssey enchantingly captures the spirit of the gathering. With nearly 100 quotations and over 100 specially created drawings, it shares and inspires new thinking and change.

Essence of Excellence

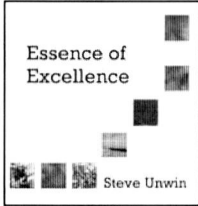

Essence of Excellence

Steve Unwin

ISBN 978-1-906420-05-5

This book is an antidote to those that claim to provide instructions for excellence.

Rather than list best practice from the past, this collection of quotations is designed to inspire the creation of the best practices of the future.

With over 180 carefully selected quotations and 130 drawings this is a book to inspire excellence in individuals and organisations.

Iran Inspired

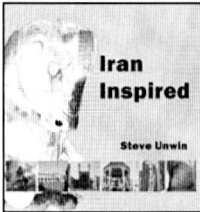

Iran Inspired

Steve Unwin

ISBN 978-1-906420-07-9

A special collection of quotations and drawings that capture some of the essence of Iran, it's people and history.

Over 120 carefully selected quotations and more than 100 drawings, create a powerful prompt for new ideas.

Beyond Best Practice - Available Soon

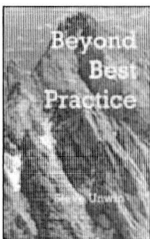

Beyond Best Practice

'…. all your knowledge is about the past and all of your questions are about the future.'

In 'Beyond Best Practice' we explore what it takes to survive and succeed in a world where the ground continuously moves from beneath your feet.

For news and special offers please visit photonbooks.com.

Corporate editions also available. A great way to energise your change program. See web site for details.